The New York Times

CROSSWORDS TO SOOTHE YOUR SOUL
75 Fun, Relaxing Puzzles

Edited by Will Shortz

ST. MARTIN'S GRIFFIN ❧ NEW YORK

All of the puzzles that appear in this work were originally published
in The New York Times from May 26, 2003, to September 5, 2003.
Copyright © 2003 by The New York Times Company.
All Rights Reserved. Reprinted by permission.

ISBN 0-312-34244-6
EAN 978-0312-34244-9

First Edition: June 2005

10 9 8 7 6 5 4 3 2 1

The New York Times

CROSSWORDS TO SOOTHE YOUR SOUL
75 Fun, Relaxing Puzzles

ACROSS
1 Was in a choir
5 All-night bash
9 Tough guys
14 Award in the ad biz
15 Genesis garden
16 "To the moon, ___!" ("The Honeymooners" phrase)
17 Much modern popular music
18 Direct
20 In the offing
22 Requisite
23 Emergency message
24 Wedding ceremony, e.g.
28 Drop from the eye
29 Wandered
33 Where fighter jets touch down
38 Shareholder's substitute
39 Wrath
40 Animal hides
42 Mincemeat dessert
43 Touches down
46 Targets of football kicks
49 Stuffed shirts
51 Derrière
52 Flier at Kitty Hawk
58 Row a boat
61 Nut
62 Unearthly
63 Be a secret author
67 "Ain't Misbehavin'" star Carter
68 Musical show
69 List-ending abbr.
70 Any Poe story
71 Improve, as text
72 Lowly worker
73 Underworld river

DOWN
1 "Hightail it out of here!"
2 Island welcome
3 More friendly
4 Speedy one-seaters
5 Gridiron official, for short
6 Hubbub
7 Captain Nemo's creator
8 Computer key
9 Convertible look-alike
10 Actor Wallach
11 Russian fighter jets
12 Canyon sound
13 New Jersey hoopsters
19 Legacy receiver
21 Regimen
25 Org. for people 50 and over
26 "Peer Gynt" composer
27 Spot for a headphone
30 Swabs
31 Escape route
32 Brunette-to-redhead jobs
33 Is under the weather
34 Tehran's locale
35 Ashcroft's predecessor
36 Negotiator with Isr.
37 One of the Fab Four
41 Whole lot
44 Wall Street index, with "the"
45 Unnatural-sounding
47 Reduce, as expenses
48 Adjusts to the surroundings
50 Glacial
53 Yawn inducers
54 Merge
55 "Super!"
56 Not flat
57 Pre-Internet communication
58 Brute
59 Pause filler
60 Wander
64 Natural tanner
65 Road cover
66 Santa's helper

by Lynn Lempel

2

ACROSS

1 Cartographers' works
5 "I did it!"
9 Count of stars on a U.S. flag
14 Canted
15 Minute bit
16 Lavatory sign
17 Gawk
18 Catskills resort, e.g.
20 Hint at
22 Magazine number
23 Azer. or Ukr., once
24 Rich source of fossil fuel
26 Utmost degree
28 Dejected
29 Land
33 Part of a circle
36 Makeup of 18-, 24-, 53- and 64-Across
39 Ned who composed "Air Music"
42 Commotion
43 Candidate of 1992 and '96
44 Component length of 36-Across
47 Inspire respect
48 Withdraws
49 Coach Parseghian
52 Mortarboard, e.g.
53 Large real estate purchase
58 Computer key
61 Flowering shrub
63 Pago Pago's locale
64 Members of Elián González's family, e.g.
67 Highly graphic
68 Camera concern
69 Inhabitant of ancient Persia
70 Launder ending
71 All the clues in this puzzle do this with 36-Across
72 Gaelic
73 Scorch

DOWN

1 Copperfield's field
2 Mission in Texas
3 Carl Reiner film "Where's ___?"
4 Witches' recitations
5 Color on the beach
6 Arranged a dinner at home
7 Walk about with a divining rod
8 Vanderbilt and Grant
9 Risky building to be in
10 India ___
11 Complain
12 Medicinal amts.
13 Calendar's span
19 Scale unit at the post office
21 Warbler Sumac
25 Passports and driver's licenses, for short
27 Nectar-pouring goddess
29 Origin suffix
30 Incantation beginning
31 Develop
32 Medieval Italian fortress city
33 Sciences' partner
34 Investment firm T. ___ Price
35 Gator's relative
37 Makes lace
38 Orange or lemon drink
40 Major util.
41 Decorated Olympian
45 Warmish
46 Okinawa honorific
50 Interstate syst.
51 Maxims
53 Cager at the Staples Center
54 Corrosive liquids
55 Milk a scene for all it's worth
56 Arterial trunk
57 Coating
58 Flunking marks
59 Schedule position
60 Cola's beginning
62 Flimsy, as an excuse
65 Capek play
66 Married name modifier

by PAtrick MErrell

ACROSS

1 Fine stone
5 Pops
10 Pelée spew
14 Reunion attendee
15 It was once advertised as "Good for tender gums"
16 He gave us a lift
17 Making of handicrafts, say
20 Pivotal
21 Getaway places
22 Neutral shade
23 Latin 101 verb
24 Gone by
26 Camp sack
27 Character in a Beatles "White Album" tune
32 "Have ___" (waiting room offer)
33 Perfect, as an alibi
37 Regan's father
38 Put a strain on
40 Paris's ___ d'Orsay
41 Ballpark figure
43 Other: Fr.
44 Certain pleasure craft
47 J.F.K. regulators
50 Same old, same old
51 House member
52 Vice President Barkley
54 Eastern priest
55 Lettuce variety
58 Object formally
62 Like tights
63 Lake rental, maybe
64 Go with
65 Hard to grasp
66 "Fun, Fun, Fun" car
67 Lens type

DOWN

1 Trunk item
2 Hand cream ingredient
3 Shirkers shirk it
4 CPR giver
5 Nod, at auctions
6 Not dismissing out of hand
7 Roast spot
8 Cape ___, Mass.
9 In a blue funk
10 Give the slip to
11 Room at the top?
12 Neighbor of Leo
13 So far
18 Draw a bead on
19 It takes two nuts
23 Kind of mushroom
24 Rose's love
25 Fasten with a belt
27 Bind with haywire
28 Partakes of
29 Nifty
30 Like a candle
31 Bromine is one
34 Gumption
35 Racer of fable
36 Bireme section
38 Prohibition: Var.
39 Fighting
42 Scene of two W.W. I battles
43 Hearing-related
45 Hue and cry
46 Won easily
47 Two-timing
48 Stag
49 Paula of pop
53 Like custard
54 Actress Anderson
55 "See you later!"
56 Not fooled by
57 Originate
59 Do something
60 Urban transport
61 Woodworker's tool

by Alan Arbesfeld

4

ACROSS

1 "Thanks for ___ Memory"
4 "Savvy?"
9 Bubble material
13 Media inits. since 1989
14 Single
15 Italian holiday
16 French lock opener
17 Last Supper question
18 Like an ancient empire
19 With 28-Down, 37-Across's autobiography
21 Fanfare
23 Serial opener
25 Cut over
26 How some messages were once sent
29 "Rob Roy" star, 1995
31 Regarding some church matters
32 High mark
33 Like Haydn's "Surprise" Symphony
36 ___ right
37 Entertainer born May 29, 1903
39 Washington, e.g.: Abbr.
40 ___ Paese cheese
41 Eastern
42 Whale watcher
43 Ones on the right
45 Slight
47 Jump on
49 Makarova of tennis
51 Click beetles
53 Noted 37-Across venue
57 One in a conger line?
58 Two chips, perhaps
60 Slangy suffix
61 Funeral stands

62 Prince Valiant's wife
63 Snap
64 Smoked fish
65 Leader of the One Israel coalition
66 37-Across's age on May 29, 2003

DOWN

1 Dash gauge
2 Spanish welcome
3 Atlas abbr.
4 Many a position in a rock band
5 Co-sign, as a loan
6 Not on the end, for short
7 Satisfied, in a way
8 Do Time?
9 Targeted, as with a mailing
10 37-Across used to emcee it
11 Big name in games
12 ___ Games
15 Certain bridge play
20 "Beowulf," e.g.
22 "Your gamblin' days ___" (Bob Dylan lyric)
24 Synchronous
26 Say too much
27 Bowl site
28 See 19-Across
30 North Carolina university
32 Harry Hershfield comic "___ the Agent"
34 Within earshot
35 Elapse
37 Wheels and deals
38 Basket material
42 Comment on a loss

44 "The Marshal of Cripple Creek" and others
45 Discontinued money
46 Polar jacket
47 William who wrote "Half Mile Down"
48 NBC's "Watching ___"
50 Winter Olympian
52 Forensic evidence collector
54 Snake dancers
55 This and that
56 City on the Brazos
59 Mobile home: Abbr.

by Jim Page

ACROSS

1 "The Fall" guy?
6 It's smaller than English
10 Temple of the Sun worshiper
14 ___ barrel
15 Load
16 Wired package
17 Actress Ina
18 Medieval armor-busting weapon
20 Printing capital
22 60's pop star Little ___
23 Holy Roman emperor
24 Verb type: Abbr.
25 Harden
26 Suffix with despond
27 One with a round head
29 Roar
31 Italian painter Reni
33 Falsified
34 It has drops and bolts
37 Young pigs
38 Investment
39 Helping theorem
40 Organ part
41 Taste
44 Simple ticket order
45 Meat in French cuisine
47 "Bathers" painter
50 Equinox mo.
51 It's in your hand
53 What each word in 18-, 20-, 34- and 51-Across could be considered
55 Not at all quiet
56 Sharpness
57 Filled treat
58 Like most planetary orbits
59 Vat preparations
60 Striking end
61 Famous

DOWN

1 Save one's sole?
2 Toyota model
3 Giant among Giants
4 "Spenser: For Hire" star
5 Kraft Foods brand
6 Sport drink put out by Coca-Cola
7 ___ the kill
8 Jane of "Coneheads"
9 Pallid
10 Dell competitor
11 One handled the same way?
12 Less dense
13 Turned, as topsoil
19 Coffee table tome, perhaps
21 Greasy organic compounds
28 Most appalling
30 Brat Pack member
31 Locale of some U.S. naval forces
32 Takes down, as a poster
33 Service area, say
34 Alms recipients
35 Modern place of entry
36 California gold rush town
37 Pie-eyed
40 Plaza
41 Vehicle with caterpillar treads
42 Not learned
43 Like apples in pies
46 Leading the pack
48 "Werewolves of London" singer, 1978
49 From the beginning: Lat.
52 Canadian Indian
54 ___ Peres (St. Louis suburb)

by Patrick Berry

6

ACROSS

1 Makes yawn
6 Sandwich shop
10 Backfire sound
14 Bullying, e.g.
15 With 34-Across, places to set pies to bake
16 Killer whale
17 ___ nova (60's dance)
18 Fender blemish
19 Watch face
20 "Is it soup ___?"
21 Third-place prize
24 Red roots in the garden
26 Maid's cloth
27 Grand ___ Dam
29 Five-pointed star
34 See 15-Across
35 Auditions, with "out"
36 Rowboat blade
37 Questions
38 Holy one
39 Animal caretakers, for short
40 Father's Day gift
41 Piano piece
42 On the ___ (close to defeat)
43 Pre-repair job figure
45 "Unto the Sons" author Gay ___
46 Band booking
47 Exterior
48 Southeastern Conference mascot
53 Towel stitching
56 "Hold on a moment!"
57 Barracks no-show
58 F.B.I. operative
60 Former Georgia senator Sam
61 Something passed in music class?
62 Discontinue
63 Where the Mets play
64 Royal Russian
65 Fund, as one's alma mater

DOWN

1 Diaper wearer
2 Relative of an English horn
3 Old, deteriorated ship
4 Feminine suffix
5 Landing strip constructors
6 Extinct flock
7 Smooth
8 Actress Kay of "Breezy," 1973
9 E-mail deliverer, with "the"
10 Store with taco shells
11 Like a dust bowl
12 March Madness org.
13 Effrontery
22 I-95, e.g.: Abbr.
23 Shoes are wiped on them
25 The "E" in B.P.O.E.
27 Orange container
28 Caravan's stopping point
29 Group of lions
30 German "a"
31 Venomous viper
32 Shoestrings
33 Shake, as an Etch A Sketch
35 Pulled tight
38 Like backwater
39 Shoe part that's wiped on 23-Down
41 Royal Arabian
42 Workaday world
44 Large lizard
45 Wed. preceder
47 Person likely to say "hubba hubba!"
48 Barley beards
49 "Nope!"
50 Rib or ulna
51 Deuces
52 Bit
54 ___ many words
55 Goulash
59 Tommy Franks, for one: Abbr.

by Gregory E. Paul

ACROSS

1 O'Neill's "Desire Under the __"
5 Peak
9 Hayloft stack
14 With 23-Across, crimson
15 Horse's pace
16 Speedy train
17 The "I" of "The King and I"
18 Not limited to roads
20 "Absolutely, guaranteed"
22 Big Apple subway, with "the"
23 See 14-Across
24 Barbecuers' equipment
28 Kind of weight
30 Queen of the fairies
33 Spooky
34 Oracle
35 Directed
36 "Definitely worth getting"
39 Beats the backside of
40 "__ Yankees"
41 Like it __
42 Award bestowed by a queen: Abbr.
43 Paper mates
44 Comfort
45 Tide alternative
46 Peter, Paul and Mary: Abbr.
47 "As a matter of fact . . ."
55 "Star Wars" weapon
56 Sporting sword
57 Wading bird
58 Self-involved
59 007
60 A bit drunk
61 Refuges
62 Raggedy fellow

DOWN

1 Cyberauction house
2 Late-night host
3 Waiter's handout
4 Attempt
5 Playing marbles
6 Flower part
7 Venus de __
8 Caesar's words to Brutus
9 Beef __ soup
10 Pungent
11 Browse (through)
12 Author Wiesel
13 __ Diego
19 Goofs
21 "Oklahoma!" aunt
24 Really irk
25 Place to kick a habit
26 Singer Cara
27 They're kissable
28 Swarms
29 Check
30 __ Carta
31 Kind of committee
32 Davis of "All About Eve"
34 Computerized photo
35 Engage in logrolling
37 Paradigms
38 Perch
43 Comely
44 Isaac and Howard
45 Early anesthetic
46 Arab chief
47 Buster Brown's four-legged friend
48 Shrek, e.g.
49 Hot rock
50 Ski lift
51 Country artist McEntire
52 Atop
53 Take care of
54 Actress Lamarr
55 Isr. neighbor

by Judy Cole

8

ACROSS

1 Meshed's land
5 R. & B. artist with the hit "Thong Song"
10 "A leopard can't change its spots," e.g.
13 Caught on a ranch
15 Baby's woe
16 Dernier ___
17 Apiarist's request on "Wheel of Fortune"?
19 Layer
20 Kind of rubber
21 Nymph of myth
23 Attention-getter
24 Land in the Seine
25 Beach memento
27 Supermodel's request on "Wheel of Fortune"?
31 Beau ___
34 Split apart
35 H+, e.g.
36 Ancient writing
37 Vendor's spot
39 Investor's channel
40 Sierra Madre treasure
41 Nordic saint
42 Conrad of old films
43 Ornithologist's request on "Wheel of Fortune"?
47 Arcade flubs
48 ___ judicata
49 Loop sights
52 Spyri heroine
54 This puzzle's request receiver
56 Propel, in a way
57 Cyclops' request on "Wheel of Fortune"?
60 Historic leader?
61 Sanitation worry
62 Verbal white flag
63 19th in a series
64 Shoulder muscles, briefly
65 E.R. cry

DOWN

1 Like a brogue
2 Bygone women's magazine
3 In a fitting way
4 Classic soft drink
5 Act opener
6 "Dies ___"
7 Have a bawl
8 Neighbor of N.Y.
9 Side of a pillowcase that a pillow goes in
10 Old Austrian money
11 Atlas stat
12 Empty talk
14 Go one way or the other
18 40 quarters, e.g.
22 It has its head in a glass
25 Espied
26 Flush, say
27 Resident's suffix
28 Big name in cheese
29 Stud site
30 S.A.S.E., e.g.
31 David of "Rhoda"
32 It replaced the 10-Down
33 Some are studded
37 Token taker
38 Cross shapes
39 Islet
41 Indebted
42 Bahamas' capital
44 Scholarship money
45 Partner of Porthos
46 Ballet leap
49 Cockpit button
50 Eric Clapton hit
51 Sport with traps
52 Clinton's birthplace
53 All ___
54 Trapper's trophy
55 Richards and Reinking
58 Bar stock
59 Tennessee athlete, for short

by Kelly Katharine Delevan

ACROSS

1 Says it's so
8 Bagel choices
15 Find and get rid of
16 "Why?"
17 & 18 Start of a query
19 How to do things
21 Terminus of Chicago's I-190
22 A long way off
23 Prince of Darkness
25 Sauternes, e.g.
26 Break down
28 River that Kazakhs call Zhayyq
29 He averaged almost a goal a game
30 Pierre's present?
31 Disruption
33 Breeder
35 & 37 Speaker of the query
41 Piedmont city
43 Big ___
44 Something brewing
45 Alphabet quartet
48 D'back, e.g.
50 "Have one"
52 Alternative to Bowser
53 Big name in wineries
54 Demands
55 Prefix with -pathy
57 Friendliness
60 & 62 End of the query
64 Stand with shelves
65 Sandal feature
66 Color lighter than crimson
67 Barely defeat

DOWN

1 Former Bush spokesman Fleischer
2 Was humiliated
3 Rake
4 Some solvents
5 Attendee
6 Franc exchange
7 Is promoted
8 Some daisies
9 Geologic division
10 Faint
11 Pituitary gland hormone
12 Much of San Bernardino County
13 Short-lived 2001 sitcom about a chef
14 Unflappable
20 Music appreciation
22 Like ___ in a poke
24 Arts patron Tully
27 Cartonful, maybe
29 A pop
32 Giant insurer
34 Angry talk
36 U.K. fliers
38 Attacks
39 Words of affection
40 Catches
42 Unmannerly
43 Tough guy star of "Love and Bullets"
45 Braggart
46 1950's Firedome
47 Perquisites
49 "All Over the World" grp.
51 Band member in "Rock 'n' Roll High School"
53 Runner
56 Competitive ___
58 Shot in the arm
59 Half of binary code
61 Kind of deposit
63 Piazza, for one

by David J. Kahn

10

ACROSS

1 Turkeys
5 Crack in the cold
9 Teatro Costanzi premiere of 1900
14 Something might suit to this
15 Prince of India
16 Super Bowl XXXIII M.V.P.
17 "What would you like in your imported coffee?" "___"
19 Piece maker
20 Campaign
21 Battle groups
23 Immunologist's concern
24 Hospitality area
25 German article
26 Swells
29 Extinguisher attachments
32 Seat of Silver Bow County
33 Elton's john
34 "Jabberwocky" start
35 Inspirations
36 Crossing cost
37 Flat topper
38 Sheds
39 Made a bird call
40 According to Miss Manners
42 Pac. borderer
43 Acting family
44 Tow away
48 "It's Too Late Now" autobiographer
50 Confidence builder
51 Ammonia derivative
52 "Would you like some more imported coffee?" "___"
54 "Delta Wedding" author
55 Jazzy James
56 Aid, in a way

57 Crosses with loops
58 Deposed king
59 Blow off steam?

DOWN

1 Bangladesh's capital, old-style
2 Flip-flop
3 Come out
4 Vacation destinations
5 Less refined
6 Duvall role in "The Godfather"
7 1977 double-platinum Steely Dan album
8 Mooches
9 Home wrecker?
10 Soap stuff
11 "Do you need anything else with your imported coffee?" "___"
12 Home overseas
13 Passing needs
18 Wise guys
22 Dirty films?
26 Cowhand's handle
27 1996 runner-up
28 Persuaded
29 Start of many addresses today
30 Man follower
31 "And would you like anything else with your imported coffee?" "___"
32 Best shots
35 Artist Edward or Thomas
36 Bankhead of old Broadway
38 Olios
39 Equal rights, e.g.
41 Statue base
42 Old quarter
44 It precedes mañana

45 Small antelope
46 Tasseled toppers: Var.
47 Stews
48 Sanyo competitor
49 Grace period?
53 Shakespearean suffix

by Randolph Ross

ACROSS

1 Vineyard fruit
6 Goes on and on
11 Pale
14 Rand McNally product
15 Cosmetician Lauder
16 Pres. Lincoln
17 Enjoy summer air-conditioning, say
19 Dieters' units: Abbr.
20 Sigma's follower
21 Right on a map
22 Frontiersman Carson
23 1970 Beatles chart-topper
27 Strikes out
29 Santa ___, Calif.
30 Cenozoic and Paleozoic
32 Brother of Cain and Abel
33 Squid's squirt
34 "Alas" and "alack"
36 Thorns' places
39 Felt bad about
41 Party list
43 The Beehive State
44 Exercise for the abs
46 African antelope
48 Southern constellation
49 ___ d'oeuvre
51 Green shade
52 Can topper
53 Washing machine cycle
56 Surgeon who pioneered the artificial human heart implant
58 Driver's need: Abbr.
59 Gymnast's feat
61 Film locale
62 "Put ___ Happy Face"

63 Be entirely satisfactory
68 "For shame!"
69 Former Chinese premier Zhou ___
70 Walkie-talkie
71 Actress Caldwell
72 Breathers
73 Guinness, e.g.

DOWN

1 Go on and on
2 Hwy.
3 Pie ___ mode
4 Page who sang "How much is that doggie in the window?"
5 Fancy homes
6 Director Spike
7 Queens's ___ Stadium
8 It precedes fast and follows farm
9 Coquettes
10 Takes up residence (in)
11 Live up to one's word
12 Hoffman who wrote "Steal This Book"
13 Hatching posts?
18 Arrogance
23 Lions' dens
24 The blahs
25 Top everything else
26 Birdie beater
28 "___, Brute?"
31 "I ___ return"
35 Not flighty
37 One of the Osmonds
38 Disreputable
40 Chad & Jeremy and others
42 Catch, as in a net
45 Suggest, as a deal

47 Big name in diamonds
50 Like ocean water
53 Fall over in a faint
54 Classic laundry detergent
55 Spikes, in volleyball
57 Up, in baseball
60 Surveyor's map
64 "___ the season . . ."
65 Altar vow
66 Lucy of "Charlie's Angels," 2000
67 Auction grouping

by Randall J. Hartman

12

ACROSS
1 Cone maker
4 "Don't you recognize the voice?!"
9 Give up, as a habit
13 Part of a Latin conjugation
15 Boarded
16 Prince William's school
17 Making trouble
19 Shiny gold fabric
20 Gabs and gabs
21 "Mercy!"
22 Permit
23 Cent
25 Glimpse
26 Away from the bow
29 Semi-colon?
30 One who walks a beat
33 Going to the dogs, e.g.
35 It's fit for a queen
37 "I feel great!"
41 Flash point?
42 "What's in ___?"
43 Sophs. two years later
44 Shade tree
46 Prefix with meter
47 That lady
50 Indian state
52 Birth-related
54 Ink spots
57 Making no sound
60 Ladies' man
61 Fancy duds
62 Neutral color
63 Like some cereals
64 Folk singer Guthrie
65 Delicate lock of hair
66 Unpromising
67 D.C. bigwig

DOWN
1 Regional groups of animal life
2 Stick on a stick
3 Nursery noisemaker
4 Composer Stravinsky
5 Duds
6 Not stand erect
7 Butted out?
8 Put the kibosh on
9 Green shade
10 Emphatic type: Abbr.
11 Hair straightener
12 Lower joint
14 Dog in Oz
18 Forwarding info on a letter
21 Rich, now
24 "Pretty nice!"
27 Big exams
28 Young 'un
30 Foldout bed
31 Lunch hour
32 Each
33 ___-de-France
34 Entrepreneur's deg.
36 Way to go: Abbr.
37 Syringe measures, for short
38 Paddle
39 Sounds of hesitation
40 Record producer Brian
45 Car owner's reference
47 Has the wheel
48 Fuss
49 ___ Howard, 1963 A.L. M.V.P.
50 Consumed with gusto
51 Three-card ___
53 Jessica of "Dark Angel"
54 Beer, informally
55 Venues
56 Yours and mine
58 Bean product?
59 Completed, as a putt
61 Weep

by Elizabeth C. Gorski

ACROSS
1 "Baywatch" beauties
6 Gulf war missiles
11 Purged
14 Water colors
15 "My Cousin Vinny" Oscar winner
16 Leb. neighbor
17 Start of a point to ponder
19 Thickness
20 Gofer
21 ". . . but is it ___?"
22 Heavenly ladle
24 Once, once
26 "That feels good!"
28 Chorus girl?
29 "The Raven" writer's monogram
31 Part 2 of the point to ponder
34 Parkinson's treatment
36 Take back
37 One waltzing Down Under
39 Now and then
43 Kind of salad
45 No-goodniks
46 Part 3 of the point to ponder
50 Point to argue
51 Half: Prefix
52 Part of E.T.A.: Abbr.
53 Strike callers
55 Medicinal syrup
57 Dander
59 Some punches
62 DVD player maker
63 End of the point to ponder
66 Perp prosecutors
67 Coffee break time, perhaps
68 Japan's second-largest city
69 Pig's pad
70 Grps.
71 She played the 10 in "10"

DOWN
1 Mexican peninsula
2 Here, in 1-Down
3 End of the line
4 Lotus-___
5 Sacramento-to-Santa Cruz dir.
6 Top banana
7 Vacation home
8 Underground org.
9 Tie
10 "Aye aye, capitán!"
11 Wee wave
12 Sea spots
13 Wood worry
18 Possesses, old-style
23 Peppermint ___ (candy purchase)
25 "Hogan's Heroes" setting
27 Five-time Derby winner
29 Nightmarish street
30 Org. for drillers and fillers
32 Chalkboard accessory
33 Country music?
35 Walk in the park, so to speak
38 Complete collapses
40 Department store department
41 Samuel's mentor
42 Atl. crosser
44 Kind of violet
46 Fair portions for the Andrews Sisters
47 Cool dude, 50's-style
48 "Makes no difference to me"
49 Lamented
54 Analyze syntactically
56 Wirehair of film
58 Radiation units
60 Superior, e.g.
61 Badlands state: Abbr.
64 Seat holders
65 10's pride

by Nancy Salomon

ACROSS

1 Lay to rest
6 Broken-off branch
10 Hydronium, e.g.
13 Expensive wrap
14 Loads
15 He talked to Wilbur Post
17 Baste over, e.g.
18 Online pastime
19 Second sock, say
20 They call New Zealand "Aotearoa"
22 It may be taken at the wrist
23 1 + 6 + 10-Across
27 Spots on diamonds
28 Rat Island group
32 Pub orders
33 Invents
36 Grant-giving grp.
37 Tag line?
38 Where a stray may stay
39 Doe and dam
40 Sportscaster Berman
41 Phrase on a Chinese menu
42 Goatish figures
43 Less calm
45 Sissy Spacek title role
46 63 + 64 + 65-Across
50 Gross part
53 Calls it quits early
54 One in an express checkout count
55 It's seen on many a roof
56 Second of three words in West Point's motto
60 Bad thing to get stuck in
61 "The __ Gave My Heart To" (1997 pop hit)
62 Piano technique improver
63 Time server
64 Piddling payment
65 Was esteemed

DOWN

1 Medit. land
2 Glaswegian denial
3 Atlanta-based station
4 Some metals
5 Good things to reap
6 "__ bleu!"
7 Body of values
8 Compete in a Soap Box Derby, e.g.
9 Discharge letters?
10 Unable to catch, with "to"
11 Kind of history
12 Mosquito guards
16 It'll barely pass you
21 W.W. II intelligence org.
22 Pro campaigners
23 Skewer
24 Mouthed off
25 Piano maintenance
26 "__ my Annabel Lee": Poe
29 O.K., in a way
30 __ Beanie Babies
31 Mouthed off to
33 Dot follower [with 38-Across + 35-Down, this puzzle's theme]
34 Suffix with vigor
35 Like Brahms's "Rain Sonata"
38 Blue books
39 City south of St. Petersburg
41 Very bright
42 To a greater extent
44 Workers skilled with tongs
45 Bull's-eye: Abbr.
47 "Bullseye!" actor
48 "Barnaby Jones" star
49 Perfectly pitched
50 A bit thick
51 Auditory
52 Nobody, slangily
55 Shot orderer
57 Screwball
58 Literary piece
59 Traffic stopper

by Patrick Merrell

ACROSS

1 They marched into toy stores in 1964
7 It looms over many actors
15 "Romanian Rhapsodies" composer
16 Fair
17 Scandinavian folklore figure in a Grieg title
19 Feel
20 Nonsense
21 It's sometimes burnt
22 1935 James Cagney crime film
23 "That stinks!"
25 Debaucher
26 Awesome
27 Cruise missile component
29 Industrial revolution elements?
30 Immobilized, as an arm
32 Senate cover-up
34 Unconfident lovers might pick them
35 Spoiled a good walk, per Mark Twain
39 Raft
41 Stripe through the target on a curling rink
42 Syndicate leaders
45 Sorting devices
47 Not needing a doctor's approval, for short
48 Zones
50 Kind of club
51 Asian sea name
52 Flag, maybe
54 Parlor game?: Abbr.
55 Royal figure of sci-fi
56 Bolt

59 Impetration
60 Coins with double-headed eagles
61 Baseball Hall-of-Famer nicknamed Turkey
62 Television tube

DOWN

1 Calm down
2 Sadistic
3 Chaffed
4 Sultan who founded an old empire
5 Prefix with tourism
6 Grouches
7 Used one's head, in a way
8 __ roll
9 Some are tied in "cho cho" fashion
10 Cute cars

11 Dial
12 Digs
13 1993 Grammy winner for "Forever in Love"
14 Awards for Stanley Ellin
18 Like seven Ryan games
24 All __
27 Crust
28 Noted Chicago journalist
31 "Troilus and Cressida" role
33 Parts
36 1959 Broadway musical that won a Pulitzer Prize for drama
37 Required
38 Hardly chic
40 Barrister's accessory

41 Choppers
42 They're sometimes mad
43 Situate
44 Overturn
46 Pole vault units?
49 Receiving a higher Consumer Reports rating, perhaps
51 Out
53 Spot
57 MapQuest offering: Abbr.
58 Ben-__

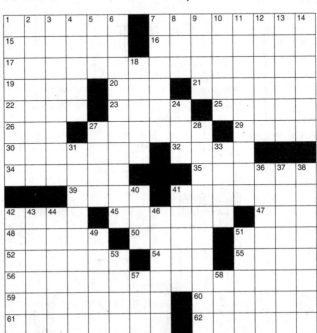

by Todd McClary

16

ACROSS

1 Hollywood snooper Hopper
6 Brought to bay
11 Winter hrs. in St. Louis
14 French cinema star Delon
15 Therefore
16 Confederate soldier, for short
17 Get on board
19 Mentalist Geller
20 Pub perch
21 Early ___ (one up at 6 a.m., say)
23 Nevada town
25 "Sweet Caroline" singer
29 "___ Like It Hot"
31 Soup eater's need
32 Vegetables that roll
33 Teacher's charges
35 Designer ___ de la Renta
37 Game show originally hosted by Monty Hall
42 Opposite of fronts
43 From east of the Urals
45 Pet protectors' org.
48 Bloodhound's clue
51 Spanish girl: Abbr.
52 1990 road film starring Nicolas Cage and Laura Dern
55 With it, 50's-style
56 N.B.A.'s Shaq
57 Bullwinkle, for one
59 Genetic info dispenser
60 Planter's tool
66 Room with an easy chair
67 Online letter
68 West Pointer
69 Radical 60's campus grp.
70 Slender and long-limbed
71 Befuddled

DOWN

1 Muslim pilgrimage
2 "Xanadu" rock grp.
3 Li'l Abner's love
4 Force
5 Writer Chekhov
6 Nickname for Leo Durocher
7 ___ room (site for a Ping-Pong table)
8 Photo blow-up: Abrr.
9 Antique French coin
10 Actress Winger
11 Literary castaway
12 Venus's sister on the courts
13 Sporty Fords, informally
18 Weed whackers
22 Awe
23 Computer key: Abbr.
24 Laze
26 Peek
27 Amount of medicine
28 Peruvian Indian
30 Erik who played Ponch on TV
34 NNW's opposite
36 Nabokov novel
38 A crow's-nest is atop it
39 Keystone site
40 Bubblebrains
41 Missing a deadline
44 Quick shuteye
45 Musketeers' weapons
46 Fastened (down)
47 Gets rid of dust bunnies
49 To wit
50 1982 Jeff Bridges film
53 Author Horatio
54 Raven-haired Puccini heroine
58 Lover's quarrel
61 Doctors' org.
62 Did a marathon
63 Unkind remark
64 Fiddle-de-___
65 Airport posting: Abbr.

by Norma Johnson

ACROSS

1 Pequod captain
5 Immense
9 Footnote abbr.
13 End of many 60's dance club names
14 Cupid
15 Bridge site
16 Sticky
17 Disgusted response
18 Did horribly on, as a test
19 "You __ here"
20 French yeses
22 "Nerts!"
24 Lazy one, slangily
26 Make unclear
27 Trifle (with)
28 Chinese drink
32 1948 also-ran
35 Talks raucously
36 Mound builder
37 Plaintive woodwind
38 One of 18 French kings
39 Good name for a Dalmatian
40 Place for a plug
41 Courted
42 Like saltwater taffy
43 Orchestral performance
45 Any ship
46 Frenchman Descartes
47 Hamilton and Burr did it
51 Cuckoo
54 Seethe
55 Eggs
56 1997 title role for Peter Fonda
57 Hazard warning
59 Farm call
61 Welsh form of John
62 Hero
63 Moran and Brockovich
64 Puppy sounds
65 Slangy denial
66 "Not on __!"

DOWN

1 Ancient market
2 Nonsense
3 ID info
4 "Hot-diggity-dog!"
5 Flavorless
6 Quantities: Abbr.
7 Exemplar of little worth
8 Delivery room surprise?
9 Natural
10 __ tie
11 "Ah, yes"
12 Like a lawn at dawn
13 1946 hit "__ in Calico"
21 180° turn, slangily
23 Tints
25 To __ (exactly)
26 Pigtail, e.g.
28 Causing to stick
29 Item for a D.J.
30 Sufficient, once
31 Lawyer: Abbr.
32 Executes
33 Web auction site
34 Bird's find
35 Pat or Daniel
38 Place of wildness, informally
39 Author Silverstein
41 "Thank heaven that's over!"
42 Onetime White House daughter
44 Primps
45 __ generis
47 Last name in mysteries
48 Sarge's superior
49 Happening
50 During working hours
51 Chop __
52 Ovid's 156
53 Bring in the sheaves
54 Betty __
58 Japanese vegetable
60 Sphere

Note: Sixteen answers in this puzzle have something unusual in common. What is it?

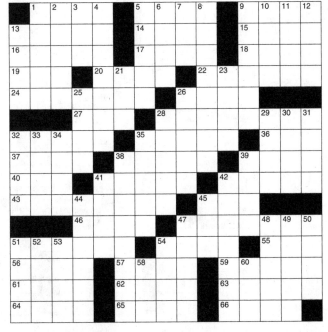

by Susan Harrington Smith

18

ACROSS

1 Where the mouth is
6 Offend
10 Exit, often
14 1975 Tony winner for Best Play
15 Hydrox rival
16 Alike, to André
17 Military brass?
18 Big screen name
19 Attend
20 They might require overtime
21 Theater usher's need
23 Stretch out
25 Jettison
26 See 53-Down
29 Protestant Reformation figure
33 Daily Planet chief
38 Harass
39 Skin cream ingredient
40 Suffix with Samson
41 Sea moss constituent
42 Ticket sales
43 "Anything Goes" composer
46 Alchemic mixture
48 Actor Jannings
49 Jewish month
51 Mailing supplies
56 Ox or pig
61 "There oughta be ___!"
62 "The Time Machine" people
63 Wrinkled, as a brow
64 Pernod flavoring
65 Aware of
66 Abstainer's opposite
67 Felt compassion (for)
68 Capitol topper
69 Clinton cabinet member Federico
70 Word that can follow the end of 21-, 33-, 43- or 56-Across

DOWN

1 Reasons to look for a shark?
2 Fit out
3 German gun
4 City on the Arkansas River
5 Enzyme suffix
6 Drudgery
7 "The Joy of Cooking" author Rombauer
8 Lavish meal
9 Front place?
10 Record holder
11 Eager
12 Standardized test topic
13 Represent graphically
21 Go smoothly
22 Baton Rouge sch.
24 Ironic
27 Home for Ulysses S. Grant
28 Championship
30 Sword part
31 Better chance
32 Bring up
33 Web site unit
34 Lod Airport carrier
35 French roast
36 Take another look at
37 Abound (with)
43 Get started
44 Tiresome one
45 Plug or play ending
47 Panhandle state: Abbr.
50 Dentist's request
52 Baccarat call
53 With 26-Across, 1912 Nobel Peace Prize winner
54 Emits coherent light
55 Garbo, by birth
56 More than a tiff
57 Food in a can
58 Freedom
59 Demeanor
60 Gillette product
64 "Won-der-ful!"

by Alan Arbesfeld

ACROSS

1 Having job security, in a way
8 Communist leader after Mao
12 Square parts
14 Where to see some clowns
15 Kitchen gizmo
16 Architect Jones
17 Musket extension?
18 St. ___ Cathedral in Londonderry
20 Descent, as of an airplane
23 Is a big burden (on)
25 Offense
26 Hard to find
27 Peace Corps cousin
29 Mother ___
30 The Hanged Man, e.g.
35 Something to shoot for
36 Math. class
37 Affect drastically
38 Heart
39 Cohort
40 Tears apart
41 Actress Graff
43 Duncan's denial
44 What a long shot faces
48 More of the answer
51 Practical joke
52 Opinion
53 Owning lots of land
54 Joseph, for one
60 About 35.3 cubic feet
61 More of the answer
62 They may need to dry out
63 Without exception

DOWN

1 Go-getter
2 Wrapped up
3 Midwest state: Abbr.
4 ___ Pass, near Pikes Peak
5 Hand-woven Scandinavian rug
6 N.Y. summer setting
7 Disappointing mark
8 Largesse recipient
9 Minneapolis suburb
10 Dry region south of Beersheba
11 Foolish
12 Scholarship criterion
13 More of the answer
14 It's illegal at some intersections
19 Some capts. are part of it
21 Edible pockets
22 More of the answer
23 Features of some apartments
24 One side in the Cod War
27 Dash
28 Dictator Amin
31 Of concern to beekeepers
32 Throwback
33 Start for step or stop
34 What passes may lead to, briefly
42 "Ha-ha," online
44 Lens
45 Half a literary leaf
46 Everglades wader
47 Mimics
49 Words on a Wonderland cake
50 Salon supply
55 Close relative
56 Kind of molecule
57 Cabinet dept.
58 West end?
59 Card game with forfeits

by Randolph Ross

20

ACROSS

1. Pennsylvania Dutch treat
11. Angry response
15. Bridge material?
16. Mineral that glistens
17. Work necessities, for some
18. Like some debaters
19. Answer to "Who wants . . . ?"
20. Singer Grant with the 1956 #1 hit "The Wayward Wind"
21. About 1% of the atmosphere
22. Sharp punches
24. Calves may wear them
27. Mont Blanc feature?
29. Some winds
30. Alphabet trio
31. "Key Largo" Oscar winner
33. Broadway aunt
35. Allegany Reservation residents
37. Extraction
41. Plug
43. Imp, say
44. Jerk
47. Oscar-winning actress Kedrova and others
49. Fine glove material
50. Be effective
53. O.E.D. stuff
54. Torpedoes
55. Kind of call
57. Two- or three-striper, briefly
58. Not docked
59. Sci-fi command site
62. Writer Berenstain famous for the Berenstain Bears

63. "Bye!"
64. Gobblers
65. Handicapping aids

DOWN

1. N.L. West team
2. Nuts and bolts
3. Half an old vaudeville duo
4. Suffix with tuber
5. ___ shui (Chinese practice)
6. Mil. rank
7. "The Right Stuff" role
8. Nearest approach
9. "___ be my pleasure!"
10. Sounds of surprise
11. Gushing flattery
12. Persist
13. Pitt and Penn
14. Common town sign
21. Certain depot
23. Put away
25. "Um . . ."
26. Offhand
28. Places
32. "Caddyshack" director
34. Updated, perhaps
36. ___ Sea, next to the Philippines
38. Like some voters
39. Battery-powered vehicle
40. Blots
42. Handheld device
44. Shocked
45. Looks after
46. Channel
48. Work of Pygmalion
51. Sheepskin leathers
52. Gets choked (up)
56. Mrs. Rabin
59. Two hearts, say
60. "O Deus, Ego ___ Te" (Latin hymn)
61. 1965 Ursula Andress film

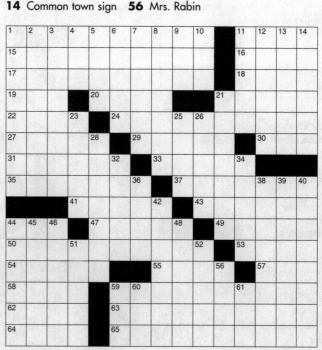

by Bob Peoples

ACROSS

1 Islamic holy war
6 Channel showing Cong. hearings
11 Transatlantic flier, for short
14 Pac-Man maker
15 Native whale-hunter
16 Toddler's age
17 Where horses drink
19 Tire filler
20 Tempest
21 Mount in Sicily
22 Show on which the Blues Brothers debuted: Abbr.
25 Sufficient
29 Make fun of
32 Elevates
33 The __ Brothers of 1960's-70's R & B
34 Treaty
35 Flipping pages
42 Ostrichlike bird
43 Magazine
44 Delicacy with Champagne
47 Certain whimsical Dutch lithographs
49 It's kneaded
51 Moscow's land: Abbr.
52 It may be due on a duplex
53 Stonehenge worshiper
56 Top flier
57 Mythical pass to the underworld
63 "The Sweetheart of Sigma __"
64 Sign before Taurus
65 Prefix with mural
66 Baseball legend Williams
67 Looks closely (at)
68 Prophets

DOWN

1 Target of a punch, maybe
2 "Give __ rest!"
3 Derby or bowler
4 Greek war god
5 Gossip
6 Rabbit's treat
7 Replay feature
8 Little, in Lille
9 Mo. before Labor Day
10 Ultimate ordinal
11 Display on a pedestal
12 Equipment near teeter-totters
13 Synagogue scroll
18 Roman Senate wear
21 Dawn goddess
22 Skirt opening
23 "Candy / Is dandy / But liquor / Is quicker" poet
24 Lollapalooza
26 "Phooey!"
27 Individually
28 Kind of acid
30 Opal or onyx
31 Gas-electric car, e.g.
34 Org. for Tiger Woods
36 "If __ a Hammer"
37 Poisoner of Britannicus
38 __Kosh B'Gosh
39 Not an abstainer
40 Knowledgeable one
41 Dame Myra
44 Christmas display
45 Poem with the story of the Trojan horse
46 Big wine holder
47 Exit
48 Avoid
49 Leaflike appendage
50 Milk giver
54 Everglades wader
55 Ready to be removed from the oven
57 Interruption
58 Prospector's prize
59 Fib
60 Western Indian
61 Dog's warning
62 Owns

by Raymond Hamel

ACROSS

1 Alternative to check or credit
5 Unrefined
10 Daedalus creation
14 Poker payment
15 "Ugh!"
16 Store sign after 9 a.m.
17 Wander
18 Really like
19 Hawaii's state bird
20 Sexologist + "The Waltons" co-star
23 Without interruption
24 Kiddy coop
28 Mtge. units
29 Short sprint
33 Picture books
34 Wish granters
36 The East
37 Film critic + "Native Son" author
41 Groceries carrier
42 Deep dislikes
43 Gap
46 "A Death in the Family" writer
47 Easter decoration
50 Third-place finisher, e.g.
52 Legend maker
54 College basketball coach + "L.A. Law" co-star
58 Pizazz
61 Scottish landowner
62 Classroom drills
63 Cockeyed
64 Refrain from children's singing?
65 Blast furnace input
66 Went really fast
67 Dummies
68 Scotch ingredient

DOWN

1 Drive-in employee
2 Sprinkle oil on
3 Union members
4 Ones who can lift heavy weights
5 Greenish blue
6 Funnyman Foxx
7 "Don't have ___, man!"
8 Deep-six
9 Aussie gal
10 Fat cat
11 Boorish brute
12 ___ state (pleasant place to be)
13 From K.C. to Detroit
21 Threw in
22 1960 chess champion Mikhail
25 Midwife's instruction
26 Broadcast
27 Code-breaking org.
30 Alicia of "Falcon Crest"
31 ___-Japanese War
32 Ibsen's Gabler
34 Become familiar with
35 Great gulp
37 Racetrack fence
38 Historic periods
39 Wish undone
40 "That is to say . . ."
41 Chinese tea
44 Samovar
45 Took a cruise
47 Writer Welty
48 Grimm girl
49 Most mirthful
51 Marsh of mystery
53 Data holder
55 Went very fast
56 The Stooges, for instance
57 Hullabaloos
58 Keebler cookiemaker
59 Chat room chuckle
60 Biggest diamond

by Norma Johnson and Nancy Salomon

ACROSS

1 "___ Poetica"
4 Build (on)
7 Money set aside
13 Doo-wop syllable
14 Wimbledon five-peater
16 Nigerian novelist Chinua ___
17 Tap-dancing without taps
19 Move unsteadily
20 Jewish month
21 Reinking on Broadway
22 Actually, legally
23 A von Trapp
25 Like paradise
27 Post-E.R. destination, maybe
28 Increase, with "up"
29 Hopscotch player's buy
33 Fla. vacation spot
36 Necessary: Abbr.
38 Tell a whopper
39 Sportage maker
40 Scalia colleague
42 "Solaris" author
43 Like some verbs: Abbr.
44 Bush adviser Karl
45 Get a little teary
47 Grade of tea
49 Mo. named for an emperor
51 Southern Conference sch.
52 Like many models
54 Chair designer Charles
57 Containing cracks, maybe
60 Liquor in a shot
62 Block brand
63 Detection devices
64 "Not to mention . . ."
66 Ultimatum words
67 Pope, 1513–21
68 Suffix with boff, in old slang
69 Comic Howie
70 "Citizen Kane" studio
71 Joined

DOWN

1 State of India
2 1970's comedy spinoff
3 Zoo alternative
4 Crunch targets
5 Qatar's capital
6 Yawn-inducing speaker
7 Have a home-cooked meal
8 Coastal highway, say
9 Marin of comedy
10 Soaks, as flax
11 U.K. awards
12 "___ #1!"
15 Like "waitperson"
18 Jiffy
24 Cassette deck feature
26 Squared
30 Worst ever
31 Stead
32 1996 veep hopeful
33 Go past
34 Get jaded
35 "Foucault's Pendulum" author
37 Iranian city
41 Picture frame shape
46 Like some talk
48 Warren Report name
50 It blows off steam
53 Detroit dud
55 Tied, as a French score
56 "Alas!"
57 Memo word
58 "___ Croft: Tomb Raider" (2001 flick)
59 Yemen's Gulf of ___
61 "Star Wars" creature
65 Prefix with skeleton

by Leonard Williams

24

ACROSS

1 Smelling salts container
5 Mooch
8 Learn in passing
14 Weaving together
16 Add
17 1955 musical version of "Cinderella"
19 Cowpunch's moniker
20 Tree whose winged seeds look like tiny canoe paddles
21 It's an honor
22 Northern Indians
24 Low ___
26 More cunning
29 Grandkids, to grandparents
30 Philosophical
32 Carlo who wrote "Christ Stopped at Eboli"
33 Roadside sign
35 Not very engaging
37 Side dish, for short
38 One who delivers papers
42 How Miss Piggy refers to herself
43 Delicacy at a state dinner?
44 Urchin's home
45 Frequently
47 Hideaway
49 Old West gunman Jack
53 Los ___
55 Fragrant ring
56 Brad Pitt thriller
57 Resulted (from)
59 Superhuman ability
61 Cockpit abbr.
62 Mission of a sort
66 Morning music
67 Wordsworth, for one
68 Casserole crust
69 Private
70 Hammock holder

DOWN

1 Checked for accuracy
2 Be essential (to)
3 Greek princess
4 Time difference
5 Judge's no-no
6 Never expressed, as tears
7 Some British imports
8 Portraitist Frans
9 Long stories
10 Revolt
11 Stay on death row
12 Start of a long-distance call
13 N.Y.C. artery, with "the"
15 Person of grace and dignity
18 Prompts grave thoughts in
23 As a result
25 Fairy-tale monster
27 By any chance
28 Set up
31 They have wedges
34 It makes an impression
36 More fancy
38 Knit shirt
39 City in central Ecuador
40 Balance
41 Sheltered spot
42 Bad start?
46 Clawed
48 Carpentry tool
50 Embodiment of a god
51 Computer key
52 Main order
54 Old Italian coppers
58 Grasped
60 Stay away from
62 She-demon
63 Lord's Prayer beginning
64 ___-pitch
65 Replayed shot

Note: A certain letter of the alphabet appears in this puzzle exactly 21 times. When you've finished solving, find and connect these letters to get an appropriate design.

by Patrick Berry

ACROSS

1 Company associated with Batman
9 "The Lion King II: ___ Pride"
15 Be sleepy
16 Huge: Fr.
17 Solo
18 Radiant
19 Like Count Basie's "darlin'"
20 Not too far gone, as cellos go
22 Numerical prefix
23 Open ___ of worms
25 Certain drags
26 XXX abroad
27 Shows
29 Cambodia's Lon ___
30 Thomas of old TV
31 Overeat
34 Principle of conservation
37 Symbol of solidarity
38 The end
39 Part of R & D: Abbr.
40 Get the gravy
44 Pack ___
45 Quit claiming
47 Elbows on the table, e.g.
48 Fill the bill?
49 They don't shoot the bull
51 Early year in Nero's reign
52 Pack animals
54 "Why Can't This Be Love" band, 1986
56 Run
57 "Don't let that get to you"
58 Assurances
59 In a sluggish way

DOWN

1 Where to split hairs?
2 Popular sports coupe
3 Last place
4 ___ Mae (Whoopi's "Ghost" role)
5 Kind of syrup
6 Like some desk trays
7 Front-line soldiers, perhaps
8 "Looky who's here!"
9 Christmas ___
10 "Good Luck, Miss Wyckoff" writer
11 Chem. unit
12 Members of a flock
13 Helium Capital of the World
14 Like mozzarella
21 D
24 Takes for a home, perhaps
26 Makes the first row of stitches in knitting
28 Things to take
30 Knits
32 1983 film romance "___ Jeunesse"
33 Indian bread
34 "Who stole the cork from my breakfast?" speaker
35 Roman carrier
36 Clean
41 Sneeze producer
42 Disclose
43 Sharp
45 Goes for
46 Name sung after "Oh" in a 1959 hit
49 Dish that's usually served with sauce
50 Like most racehorses
53 Mayo, for instance
55 Equal

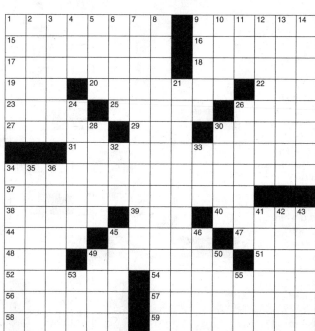

by Manny Nosowsky

26

ACROSS

1 Fashionable
5 Where bats "hang out"
9 Triangular traffic sign
14 Sweep under the rug
15 Like droughty land
16 Typo
17 Neck and neck
18 Lion's locks
19 Popular dip for 48-Down
20 Gain wealth opportunely, in a way
23 "Two Mules for Sister ___" (1970 film)
24 Three, on a sundial
25 "That feels good!"
28 Snake that may warn before it strikes
31 Harper Valley grp., in song
34 Lock of hair
36 "___ was saying . . ."
37 Any day now
38 Nickname in James Fenimore Cooper tales
42 Artist Warhol
43 Vintner's tank
44 Cruise ship
45 Put into words
46 Hot pepper
49 Give it a whirl
50 Little League field surface, probably
51 Stethoscope holders
53 She played TV's Amanda Woodward
61 Shake hands (on)
62 Per person
63 ___ Major

64 More vigorous
65 Suffix with buck
66 Appearance
67 Be head over heels about
68 Prospectors' receptacles
69 Tiptop

DOWN

1 Bake-off figure
2 Honey factory
3 "The very ___!"
4 Piggy bank filler
5 Tourist's take-along
6 Where Noah landed
7 Chianti or Soave
8 Place of bliss
9 Boot camp affirmative
10 Tehran resident
11 Writer ___ Stanley Gardner

12 Profit's opposite
13 "Darn!"
21 Severe
22 "Old MacDonald" refrain
25 World Almanac section
26 Madison Square Garden, e.g.
27 Exciting
29 One of the senses
30 "Saving Private Ryan" craft: Abbr.
31 Score unit
32 Laser printer powder
33 Hopping mad
35 Hog's home
37 Go downhill fast?
39 Dodge
40 Element of hope?
41 Pencil pusher
46 Stick together

47 Converted liberal, informally
48 Mexican snacks
50 Beef animal
52 Losing streak
53 "That is so funny"
54 "Goodness gracious!"
55 Guthrie who sang at Woodstock
56 Harvest
57 Zhivago's love
58 New York's ___ Canal
59 Toward the big waves
60 Captain, e.g.

by Gregory E. Paul

ACROSS
1 An American in Paris, maybe
6 "By ___!"
10 Sch. groups
14 Edwin in Reagan's Cabinet
15 "Excuse me . . ."
16 Pathetic
17 Stupefied
18 Superman's mother
19 Board member, for short
20 Summer retreat
23 Silhouette
24 Annoyance
25 With deliberate hamminess
28 Player's club?
29 N.Y.C. subway
32 More slippery, perhaps
33 Break bread
34 Middling
35 Summer retreat
39 Author Dinesen
40 "I want my ___!" (1980's slogan)
41 Sword handles
42 ___ Paul guitars
43 Gossip
44 Mocks
46 Shoveled
47 Initial venture
48 Summer retreat
54 Promotable piece
55 Fictional detective Wolfe
56 Dangerous gas
57 Babysitter's headache
58 Perón and Gabor
59 Work often read before the "Odyssey"
60 Compos mentis
61 Lone
62 Euro fractions

DOWN
1 Actor Jannings
2 TV's leather-clad princess
3 Busiest
4 At this very moment
5 Bit of summer attire
6 Bucket of bolts
7 Midway alternative
8 "Billy Budd" captain
9 Grossly underfeed
10 Naval Academy freshman
11 Travel before takeoff
12 "Right on!"
13 Very short wait, in short
21 Film producer Roach
22 Workmanship
25 Polite
26 Build ___ against (work to prosecute)
27 Layered minerals
28 Bit of luggage
29 Cries one's eyes out
30 Sporty Mazda
31 Romantic rendezvous
33 Letter container: Abbr.
34 Story that might include a dragon
36 Conceives of
37 Gambling site, briefly
38 Flamboyantly overdone
43 Astronaut Grissom
44 Humorous
45 Suffix with ranch
46 "Inferno" poet
47 Not domesticated
48 Poet Teasdale
49 McGregor of "Down With Love"
50 "Whip it" band
51 Tennis score after deuce
52 Bearded animal
53 Leaves off
54 "Nova" network

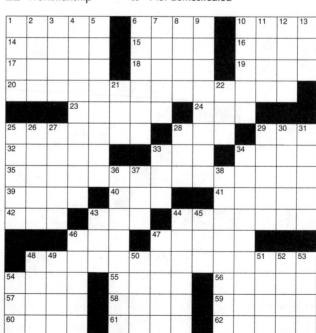

by Karen M. Tracey

ACROSS

1 Sidelines shout
4 One appearing between numbers
9 Greek marketplace
14 "___ pig's eye!"
15 Old Pisa dough?
16 Deadly snake
17 Definition of 41-Across
20 Joshes
21 Jones of the Miracle Mets
22 Bib. prophet
23 Definition of 41-Across
27 Sweater material
29 Caffeine source
30 Actor Wallach
31 Pleasing view
35 Doofus
39 Mountains crossed by Hannibal
41 Theme of this puzzle
43 Property claim
44 Corrective eye surgery
46 Straight from the keg
48 Cross shape
49 Berlin Airlift grp.
51 Foes of Carthage
53 Definition of 41-Across
59 W.W. II sphere: Abbr.
60 Hard to get to know
61 Neighbor of Minn.
64 Definition of 41-Across
68 Josh
69 "He's ___ nowhere man . . ." (Beatles lyric)
70 Beehive State native
71 Eagerness
72 Gossipmonger
73 No-show's test score

DOWN

1 Classic Parker Brothers game
2 Prefix with lock or knock
3 Travails
4 Tarzan portrayer Ron
5 Near the center of
6 "Photographs & Memories" singer
7 Quarter back?
8 Ruhr Valley city
9 Pennsylvania and others
10 Jazz arranger Evans
11 Microscope lens
12 Witherspoon of "Legally Blonde"
13 Tapestry
18 Where pomelos grow
19 Derisive shout
24 Louis ___, the Sun King
25 Source of embarrassment
26 Table salt formula
27 Banquet
28 ___ podrida
32 Jack of "Barney Miller"
33 Wine cask
34 Lizard's nibble
36 Like commando raids
37 Bad-tempered
38 ___ probandi (burden of proof)
40 Beget
42 Mend
45 Person with a paddle
47 Detachable craft
50 Tab site
52 Like 1950's recordings
53 Hostess Perle
54 Lupine : wolf :: lutrine : ___
55 WarGames" setting
56 "Forget it!"
57 Orléans's river
58 A lot
62 When the witches first appear in "Macbeth"
63 Ship's backbone
65 Equal: Prefix
66 Magician's prop
67 Where I-10 and I-95 meet: Abbr.

by Barbara Olson

ACROSS

1 Faucet part
5 Kites, e.g.
10 N.B.A. nickname
14 Dodeca- halved
15 Company that made Asteroids
16 Where Pearl City is
17 Picketer, perhaps
18 Virologist Salk
19 Chinese dynasty up to A.D. 1125
20 Result of a banner getting stripped?
23 Noun concerning verbs
24 Grand Bahama, e.g.
25 Kind of nut
28 Skill
29 Christian singer Grant
32 On account of
34 Result of "cabbage" getting moldy?
38 Nobelist Hahn or Warburg
41 1972 Derek and the Dominos hit
42 Sports achievement award
43 Result of a farm animal losing opacity?
46 Fajita flavorer
47 Delicacy from the sea
48 Curative locale
51 Knock out
52 Way to Roosevelt Island
56 Whiplike?
58 Result of a dairy food getting larger?
62 Sanction
64 Stars, in Kansas' motto
65 Abounding
66 Miniature cloud
67 Reds Hall-of-Famer Tony
68 Prayers to Mary
69 Recent
70 Vermont ski resort
71 Like cranberries

DOWN

1 Kind of daisy
2 Cloth-stretching frame
3 Still around
4 Underground conduits
5 Low, in La Paz
6 "Believe ___ . . ."
7 Actress Oakes of "CHiPs"
8 Olive ___
9 Cordage fiber
10 Undivided
11 Absolutely smooth
12 "Got it!"
13 ___ vadis
21 Expensive
22 More than patch up
26 The Miners of the Western Athletic Conf.
27 Warranting an R, perhaps
30 Gibson and Brooks
31 "Good going!"
33 One to whom a warranty applies
34 Functions properly
35 Comic Louis
36 Part song
37 Uncommonly good
38 Mount near Mt. Olympus
39 Loosen up
40 Air on the tube
44 Crown
45 If not
48 Cannabis ___ (marijuana)
49 Favor
50 Not moving
53 Gains grains
54 Good point
55 Part of MGM
57 Charlotte Corday's victim
59 Ballyhoo
60 Shot up
61 Level
62 Harry Potter's Hedwig, for one
63 Asian auto import

by Cathy Millhauser

30

ACROSS

1 Unknown quantity
8 Pet felines
15 Two-year stretches
16 Sent, in a way
17 Stumping
18 Flushes
19 Wood sugar
20 One who might be put away
21 "You mean, this isn't waterproof?"
23 Title character in a 1986 Woody Allen film
27 Watch, say
32 Setting for William Tell
33 Sped off
34 Mother of Levi and Judah
35 Houston and others
37 Person with something to hide
39 Noted portrait subject of Hans Holbein the Younger
41 Warehouse
42 Proceeds
44 "Catch!"
45 Choose
46 They're easily bruised
49 Filibuster
51 Linda of "Jekyll & Hyde"
52 Like many movies nowadays
54 Head home
59 Not neat
62 Three-walled court activity
63 Sound made by a rapper
64 Rembrandt and Picasso
65 No easy trips
66 China cabinet displays

DOWN

1 Microsoft product introduced in 2001
2 Open
3 Repast
4 Catch or latch follower
5 Perfect accord
6 Like some golf courses
7 Mattress feature
8 Actress Austin of "Knots Landing"
9 Grable's co-star in "Moon Over Miami"
10 Unwanted emanations
11 Try to buy, as at Sotheby's
12 France's Belle ___
13 Still, in verse
14 Grp. in 60's news
20 Queens plate setting
22 Sworn secrecy
24 Eggnog need
25 First name in conducting
26 Audio problems
27 Arks
28 Suggest
29 Back up again, as a disk
30 Telltale ___
31 Billy's nickname
36 North Carolina county
38 Fixed
40 Consign
43 Like fine cigars
47 Baggage handler
48 Symphony that premiered in Vienna in 1805
50 Storybook ending?
53 November honorees
55 Dismissive remarks
56 On the quiet side
57 Pastry server
58 Meeting of heads?
59 Hosp. areas
60 Hoover, briefly
61 Old verb ending
62 Kind of fuel

by Elizabeth C. Gorski

ACROSS

1 Karate blow
5 Microscope part
9 Separates, as flour
14 Super-duper
15 Baseball's Moises or Felipe
16 Dunderhead
17 Poker holding lower than three-of-a-kind
18 Oscar winner Patricia
19 Big
20 Punish action star Norris?
23 Superlative suffix
24 "Anchors Aweigh" grp.
25 CPR expert
26 "Moby Dick" whaler
28 Lipton competitor
30 Hurrying
33 Parts of gowns that go over the shoulders
36 Detroit baseballer
37 Titled lady
40 Massage
42 Fast jets, briefly
43 Alex Haley saga
45 River in a Strauss waltz
47 Spills clumsily
49 Big name in small planes
53 Close by
54 Letters before an alias
55 Balloon filler
56 High-jumper's hurdle
58 Rely on comic Keaton?
62 In the sky
64 Delhi dress
65 "Well done!"
66 Roast host
67 The dark force
68 Miners' finds
69 Worker with autumn leaves
70 Dicker
71 Toward the sunset

DOWN

1 Kid's pistol
2 Like laryngitis sufferers
3 Whopper toppers
4 Lima's locale
5 Acquire slugger McGwire?
6 Put into office
7 Biblical ark builder
8 "Star Trek" navigator
9 Formal headgear
10 Actress Lupino
11 Dismiss gangster Moran?
12 Clothing
13 Proofreader's "leave it"
21 Hair removal brand
22 Jail, slangily
27 Crops up
29 Fearsome fly
30 "No man ___ island . . ."
31 Ready
32 "48 ___" (Nick Nolte film)
34 "No ifs, ___ or buts!"
35 Sweet ___ (flower)
37 E.R. workers
38 "You've got mail" co.
39 Drop drawers on actor Hudson?
41 Avoid President Clinton?
44 Break into bits
46 Boyfriend
48 Goof up
50 Lampoon
51 Sisters' daughters
52 Collar
54 Skylit lobbies
56 30's boxing champ Max
57 ___ mater
59 Like Goodwill goods
60 Prepare for a rainy day
61 Falling flakes
63 Membership charge

by Nancy Salomon and Harvey Estes

ACROSS

1 Civil rights org.
6 Madame Bovary
10 Choice on "Let's Make a Deal"
14 Come to pass
15 Castle defense
16 Henry VIII's second or fourth
17 1954 movie starring 25- and 44-Across
20 Storm center
21 Kelly's possum
22 "I swear!"
23 Worth a C
24 Half of a sawbuck
25 Half of a famous comic duo
29 Tibetan priest
33 Jennifer Garner spy series
34 Bachelor's last words?
35 Rah-rah
36 Some auction bids
37 Arsonist, e.g.
39 Grin from ear to ear
40 Blunted blade
41 William Halsey, e.g.: Abbr.
42 Marilyn Monroe's real first name
43 Virgin Is., e.g.
44 Half of a famous comic duo
47 Sheepcote
48 Beanery sign
49 Source of mohair
53 Diner handout
54 ___ alai
57 1956 movie starring 25- and 44-Across
60 Kind of page
61 Skin soother
62 It comes from the heart
63 Desires

64 A bit less than a meter
65 Steadfast

DOWN

1 Musical mark
2 "___ Breaky Heart" (1992 hit)
3 Farm measure
4 Pool tool
5 Takes care of charges ahead of time
6 Political refugee
7 Like early LP's
8 Periodical, for short
9 Kansas town famous in railroad history
10 Mend, in a way
11 Story starter
12 Burden of proof
13 Musical mark

18 Muddy up
19 Charged particle
23 "George of the Jungle" star Brendan
24 Generic pooch
25 A singing Jackson
26 Run off to wed
27 Bill tack-on
28 One of the Flintstones
29 Hercules had 12
30 Turn away
31 Orange Bowl city
32 Jingle writer
37 Backward-moving basketball shot
38 Delightful place
42 Musical mark
45 Had to have
46 ___-war bird
47 Act the snoop
49 "Hey, sailor!"
50 "Uh-uh"

51 Campbell of country
52 GM line
53 Othello was one
54 Trial group
55 "The Thin Man" dog
56 Emphatic type: Abbr.
58 Plug or pay ender
59 Ghost's cry

by Roy Leban

ACROSS

1 Fermentation receptacle
4 Aromatic salves
9 Rough, as a car engine
14 Rabin's land: Abbr.
15 Enjoyed immensely
16 Loosen, as laces
17 Long-ago battle protection
19 Klutzy
20 Annual July sports event with the world's largest live audience
22 Cookbook author Rombauer et al.
23 ___ sauce
24 Co. badges
27 Playing dirty tricks
28 Should, with "to"
31 Part of a parcel
32 "Peter Pan" dog
33 Shortly
35 Lance Armstrong, at the end of the 2003 20-Across
39 Batman's home
40 Daredevil Knievel
41 End-of-the-week cry
42 Slowly merged (into)
44 Moves it, informally
48 Key futilely pushed after a computer freeze
49 Kind of hand
50 One must be quick to join it
51 Winner's prize, in 20-Across
55 Ruler of a hive
58 "Janie's Got a Gun" rock band
59 UPS shade
60 Catches
61 From Okla. City to Houston
62 Pantywaist
63 "Uncle Tom's Cabin" girl
64 Novelist Josephine

DOWN

1 Muggee, e.g.
2 Toward the beach
3 Emotional damage
4 Cigar wraps
5 "Look ___!"
6 Table extender
7 ___ Woods National Monument
8 Big media to-do
9 Like good oranges
10 Feminine suffix
11 31-Down plan: Abbr.
12 Laotian money
13 So far
18 Ayatollah's land
21 Saw
24 SALT topic
25 Job for a plumber
26 Match unit
28 Hot bowlful
29 Prefix with sphere
30 Pool and darts
31 Driver's aid: Abbr.
32 Big lobby in D.C.
34 Montreal is in it: Abbr.
35 Frequent San Francisco conditions
36 Related to: Suffix
37 Like some TV channels, briefly
38 Last moment to prepare
39 Old inits. in telecommunications
43 Cry after a long wait
44 Start of an idea
45 More than urge
46 Sub-Saharan pest
47 Willie Mays phrase
49 Copper
50 Unkempt
51 Fir trees
52 Wine: Prefix
53 Shawl, e.g.
54 Bends, as in a river
55 Gridiron V.I.P.'s
56 Mentalist Geller
57 Canon camera model

by Patrick Merrell

ACROSS

1 Like an ass
7 Field call
10 Scrap
13 Clodpate
14 "___ quiet!"
15 It may be involved in a shell game
16 Thresher shark
17 IHOP offering
19 Signal, in a way
21 Brimless hat
22 Some jazz performances
26 First Indian P.M.
28 Old pro
29 Outfit
31 Dramatist Peter who won a Tony for "Marat/Sade"
33 Skill at picking up things?
34 One way to get to Washington
36 Spontaneously
38 With 14-Down, feature of this puzzle repeated three times
42 Jazz dance
43 How coffee may be served
45 Form of music files on the Net
48 Much of the Beatles' "She Loves You"
50 Kind of oven
51 Tel ___
53 Bite, say
55 Weizman of Israel
56 Aspect
58 Cannot stand
60 Direction indicator of the earth's magnetic field
62 Regular employment
67 Actor Chaney
68 Janet Jackson hit "___ Lonely"

69 Part of the iris
70 Old Spanish queen
71 Washington agent
72 Many a marathon winner

DOWN

1 Noisy transports
2 N.Y. neighbor
3 Co-star of Liam in "Les Misérables," 1998
4 World financial grp.
5 It precedes one
6 BP competitor
7 Half of table salt
8 Org. popular with authors
9 Cried
10 Unclear
11 Comes back
12 Begin
14 See 38-Across

18 Nudge
20 It might get your feet wet
22 Clampett of 1960's TV
23 Soft shade
24 Chew (over)
25 Potted plant sites
27 Org. that raises a racket?
30 Minor
32 Crunch
35 Sneaks, say
37 Misrepresent
39 Gave off
40 Tease
41 Medium, e.g.
44 Some goo
45 IHOP offering
46 Land of the Blessed, in myth
47 Llama relative
49 Principal location?: Abbr.

52 Annoy
54 Brownie maker
57 Letters of relief
59 Infrequent
61 ___-appropriate
63 It's worth about a penny
64 Rapture
65 Suffix with schnozz
66 Embargo

by Michael Shteyman

ACROSS
1 Gets rid of, as a hangover
10 Coup group
15 What folks are saying
16 Name referenced in Jefferson Airplane's "White Rabbit"
17 Gets worse
18 Certain sorority member
19 Sign of summer
20 Dead giveaways?
22 Tad
23 Shade
25 Dejected
26 Golfer Ballesteros
27 Abbr. in many court citations
29 Armless seat
31 Library sign
33 Sources
34 Cactus flower eater
36 Boxing champ whose autobiography was titled "A Man Must Fight"
37 Some "Star Wars" roles
38 1998 film based on a Chinese folk tale
39 Goes back to zero, say
41 Snug retreats
45 "Young Frankenstein" woman
46 Tropical forest vine
48 ___ Maar, Picasso subject
49 Philips of stand-up fame
50 London fog
52 Pen point
53 Pre-Xerox copy
55 Flavor-intensifying compound
57 Square
58 Surgical tool
59 Stillness
60 Subjects of King Sargon

DOWN
1 Sylphlike
2 Come unglued
3 Record holders?
4 Org. launched by Nixon
5 Kind of position
6 Contraction
7 Sailing
8 Run-down theater
9 Two-___ (aggressive)
10 Reprobates
11 Black and tan ingredient
12 "The Family Circus" cartoonist
13 Pastime
14 Biggest stories
21 Check-out limit?
24 #1 instrumental hit of 1958
26 Untouchable
28 Squares
30 Pulp creation of Robert E. Howard
32 Pump liner
34 Mesabi Range excavation
35 Traditional site of Jesus' crucifixion
36 They're good at hits
37 Wizened
38 It may be spotted in kindergarten
40 Sildenafil citrate, commonly
42 Series of movements
43 Large spiral shell
44 They have duel purposes
47 "Mexicali Rose" singer
50 Tiara wearer
51 Jack of old TV
54 Foible
56 Baby Bell competitor

by Patrick Berry

36

ACROSS
1 Spellbound
5 Homer epic
10 Early baby word
14 Ibiza, e.g., to Spaniards
15 Mother-of-pearl
16 Not new
17 Extended family
18 Unique
20 Chilling out
22 Behind a wrecker, say
23 Actor with the catchphrase "I pity the fool!"
24 Picks out in a lineup, for short
27 In-flight info
28 Eight: Prefix
32 Uncle of old TV
34 Boneless chicken pieces
37 Wise __ owl
38 Satisfying close . . . or what 20- and 55- Across have in common?
41 Gazillions
42 Port of southern Italy
43 Some French Impressionist paintings
46 Nothin'
47 Life story
50 "Indeed!"
51 Notes after dos
53 Moves like a dragonfly
55 Not going anywhere
59 1950's-60's adolescent
62 Same, in Somme
63 Augury
64 "Breakdown ahead" warning
65 "Good shot!"
66 Metal in some batteries
67 Wards (off), as an attack
68 Brown quickly

DOWN
1 1980's-90's hitmaker Lionel
2 Leaning
3 Farms with banana trees
4 Fiery ballroom dance
5 Home __ (near)
6 Singer k. d. __
7 Reykjavik's home: Abbr.
8 Forster's "__ With a View"
9 Bend out of shape
10 John Wayne nickname
11 "Just __ suspected!"
12 TV room
13 Do sums
19 Spumante region
21 "Forget it!"
24 "Nothing to worry about . . ."
25 Corner-to-corner: Abbr.
26 Capitol V.I.P.: Abbr.
29 401, to Nero
30 Change for a 20
31 Radio City Music Hall fixture
33 Reclined
35 Suffix with Rock
36 Actress Ward
38 Polar bear's transport?
39 Actor Beatty
40 Alternative to a volunteer army
41 "Little Women" woman
44 Chicago paper, for short, with "the"
45 Trigger
48 Cornell's home
49 Horse farm hand
52 "Lifted"
54 They may be placed on a house
55 In __ (coordinated)
56 Classic supermodel
57 Dweeb
58 Some coll. tests
59 Dickens's pen name
60 French friend
61 London's Big __

by Elizabeth C. Gorski

ACROSS

1 Lettuce variety
5 "La Vie en Rose" singer Edith
9 From way back
14 Available to serve
15 Fruit with wrinkled skin
16 Zellweger of "Chicago"
17 Fruit plate item
19 Saltine brand
20 Buys off
21 Jackson 5 member
23 Coffee-to-go need
24 Whom a coach coaches
25 Overcharge
26 Diner sign
27 Broth shortcut
30 States further
33 Humor magazine since 1952
34 Word reference pioneer
35 ___-Magnon
36 Spike Lee's "Summer of ___"
37 Mom-and-pop grp.
39 Medical plan, for short
40 Transcribers' goofs
42 Battery size
43 British gun
44 Ben & Jerry's offering
48 Blow off steam
49 Fitzgerald forte
50 Snigglers' prey
53 Roth ___
54 Saxophonist Stan
55 Fix in a cobbler's shop, say
57 Impression
59 Theme of this puzzle, so to speak
61 Between the lines
62 Golden rule word
63 2002 Eddie Murphy film
64 Inuit transports
65 "Hey you!"
66 Place-kickers' props

DOWN

1 Long, high pass
2 Not active, chemically
3 Contradict
4 African trees with thick trunks
5 Bars of Avon
6 Foot store chain inits.
7 In sum
8 Befitting a son or daughter
9 Petite pasta
10 Contingency ___
11 Blitz
12 1960 Everly Brothers hit
13 Determined to have
18 Verne's reclusive captain
22 Ali vs. Liston outcome, 1964
25 Thailand, once
26 Prefix with management
28 Thurman of "Pulp Fiction"
29 Guns rights org.
30 They've got issues
31 Corn flakes or raisin bran
32 Atone
36 Ukr. or Lith., once
37 Treaty
38 Lao-tzu's "___ Te Ching"
41 Columbus Day mo.
42 Hippolyta's warriors
43 Deems it appropriate (to)
45 Language suffix
46 Goes haywire
47 Cry out for
51 Freewheeling
52 Ski run
54 Comes down with
55 Urban disturbance
56 Häagen-Dazs alternative
58 Half brother of Tom Sawyer
60 Capt.'s inferiors

by Harvey Estes

38

ACROSS

1 Word in many farm names
6 [Look over here!]
10 "___ Apart" (2003 film)
14 Bear market direction
15 Like some league games
16 Singer Horne
17 Quickly, to an egotist?
20 Not on board, maybe
21 Poverty
22 Zero
23 One in a suit
25 Determines the age of
27 It may be sealed
30 Put away
31 Fail to stop on a dime?
33 Garfield's foil
35 Kind of party
40 Toast made by an egotist?
43 Fell back
44 ___ lily
45 May event, for short
46 Cheer competitor
49 Ham, to Noah
50 Used a fruit knife
53 ___-Roman
55 Summer cooler
56 "Back in the ___"
59 Bursts
63 Egotist's favorite person?
66 Deep-six
67 Uncreative learning method
68 Move (over)
69 Clinches, as a victory
70 Class identification
71 Brains

DOWN

1 Where SARS originated
2 Reasons to vote no
3 Crime novelist Rendell
4 Underlying character
5 Everest guide, often
6 Pen ___
7 Pen group
8 Lucid
9 Young 'un
10 1936 candidate Landon
11 Intended
12 Meg's "Sleepless in Seattle" role
13 Things at one's fingertips?
18 Flatfoot's circuit
19 Rare find
24 Second-in-command
26 "See you 'round"
27 Danish physicist Niels
28 ___ fixe
29 Tabloid fodder
31 Breaking pitch
32 Many wedding guests
34 Spooky
36 Lyric poem
37 Barroom sticks
38 Jason's ship
39 Heraldic beast
41 Parody
42 Beside oneself
47 Natural breakwater
48 On the opposite bank
50 Page of music
51 Temporary, as a committee
52 Baseball's Pee Wee
53 Actress Garbo
54 Shot glass capacity, roughly
57 Nimble
58 ___ gin
60 Lowly laborer
61 General ___ chicken
62 Net-surfer's stop
64 Dunderhead
65 "___ the glad waters of the dark blue sea": Byron

by Norm Guggenbiller

ACROSS

1 Base transportation
5 Rice in a bookstore
9 Nobel-winning peacemaker
14 Conductor Klemperer
15 Pass
16 White poplar
17 No matter what
19 Asian tree with many trunks
20 Comparatively cracked
21 Sorrows
22 It's intoxicating
23 National Aviation Hall of Fame site
25 Film festival film, often
28 It's taken in for treatment
29 Spring's opposite, oceanwise
32 Shoppers' pursuits
33 Joe Hardy's temptress, on Broadway
34 Its slogan was once "The sign of extra service"
35 Balmoral relative
36 Feller of folklore?
37 Uncommon insight
38 Mounted on
40 League: Abbr.
41 Lug
43 AWOL
44 Jupiter, e.g.
45 Olympian
46 Time out
48 CD follower
49 Visual
51 Kicks downstairs, so to speak
55 Echo location
56 Where cons may congregate
58 Steelhead or squaretail
59 Saint known as "the Great"
60 Talker with a beak
61 Antônio, for one
62 It's spun
63 Request

DOWN

1 Rivers with barbs
2 Famed words to a backstabber
3 Louisiana, e.g., in Orléans
4 Bun alternative
5 Be like-minded
6 Film genre
7 It has a peacock logo
8 Peacock plume feature
9 Wooden footwear
10 Marine rock-clinger
11 Live ascetically
12 Garden spray
13 Top scores, sometimes
18 A ton
21 "Knockin' on Heaven's Door" singer, 1973
23 Greek god of wine
24 Detective Pinkerton and others
25 Item on a chain
26 "Swell!"
27 Sky Masterson's creator
28 Good things
30 Good thing
31 Shade of red
36 Supreme Court middle name
39 Leave rubber on the road
41 Remote option
42 Potential source of verbal misunderstanding
47 Poem division
48 Amber, e.g.
49 Fall times: Abbr.
50 Irene of "Fame"
51 Christian from France
52 "The Best Man" star Diggs
53 Shore soarer
54 Admission of 1889: Abbr.
56 Use diligently
57 Mens ___ (criminal intent)

by Robert H. Wolfe

ACROSS

1 1993 De Niro title role
7 Hedger's answer to "Have you done your homework?"
15 Site of Syria's Great Mosque
16 Flag-waver's event?
17 Suez Canal nationalizer
18 Space program
19 Enfant terrible
20 Dance in the streets
22 Old lady, backwoods-style
23 Patch target
25 Goose
26 Dreamcast maker
27 Ignominy
29 "Scram!"
30 Sound system control
31 Place to get a buzz?
34 Where Ashur was the supreme deity
35 Ties together
39 Wind down
41 Title role for Daly
44 Unsubstantial stuff
45 For this reason
46 Nebraska county whose seat is Nebraska City
47 Jerusalem artichoke, e.g.
49 Those, to Muñoz
50 Originally
51 Divided differently, in a way
53 Ending with form
54 Member of the legume family
56 C.P.A.'s concern
58 Arugula alternative
59 "Swan Lake" heroine
60 Intensified
61 Broke down in school

DOWN

1 Churchill is in it
2 Shady strolling spots
3 Is ready to give up the ship
4 They result in two outs: Abbr.
5 Abbr. on some dials
6 Bridge maven
7 Kind of temple
8 For all to see
9 Soul singer Lattisaw
10 Sped
11 Food scraping
12 Cultivated
13 Part of the Quaternary Period
14 William Shatner novel
21 Fitting activity?
24 "A Raisin in the Sun" actress
26 Pillsbury competitor
28 Like the month of May?
30 Take the wrong way?
32 Narrow inlet
33 Suffix for a bibliophile
36 Refers to
37 Intensify
38 Wasn't steady
40 Put out of bounds, so to speak
41 Ached
42 Not taut
43 Drive
47 Part of a dovetail
48 Put a new surface on
51 Unusually excellent
52 Man Ray's movement
55 Like some churches: Abbr.
57 Generation ___

by Sherry O. Blackard

ACROSS

1 Kiss
6 Tool building
10 Butcher's or bakery
14 Process in a blender
15 Sampras or Rose
16 Place to see 20th-century paintings in N.Y.
17 Philanthropist Brooke ___
18 Grad
19 Sign on a store door
20 "Royal" action film, 2002
23 "___ Haw"
24 Yo-yo or Slinky
25 Corsage flower
29 Brother of Abel
31 "Camelot" president, for short
34 U.S. Grant's foe
35 Angel's headgear
36 Prefix with commuting
37 "Royal" Bogart/Hepburn film, 1951
40 Knife handle
41 Grades 1-12, for short
42 Let loose, as pigs
43 No longer used: Abbr.
44 Over hill and ___
45 Like bread dough
46 Brief instant
47 Hurry
48 "Royal" film based on a classic children's story, 1974
57 Maui dance
58 Nest eggs for seniors: Abbr.
59 Bottled water from France
60 Egyptian fertility goddess
61 On-the-hour radio offering
62 Extremely successful, slangily
63 Old Iranian leader
64 Heredity carrier
65 Deuce takers

DOWN

1 Small fight
2 Sled dog command
3 Johnson of TV's "Laugh-In"
4 Corporate heads, for short
5 Woman's head cover
6 Extra
7 Aid
8 Needle case
9 Drop from major to captain, say
10 Great ___ Mountains National Park
11 Pueblo Indian
12 Augur
13 Sharp pain, as from hunger
21 Multivolume ref.
22 Oui's opposite
25 Right: Prefix
26 Addict's program, in short
27 Heads of staffs?
28 Furnace output
29 Hidden stash
30 Jai ___
31 Army vehicles
32 Navy unit
33 Singer Rogers
35 San Francisco's Nob ___
36 Sandwich fish
38 Responding (to)
39 Most odd
44 Agnus ___
45 Puppy sound
46 /
47 "Steppenwolf" author
48 1950's TV's "___ Is Your Life"
49 Silence
50 Director Kazan
51 Elm or oak
52 Place for an Easter egg hunt
53 Songwriter Novello
54 Kindly
55 Like dry mud
56 Genesis grandson

by Andrea Carla Michaels

42

ACROSS

1 Letters that lack stamps
6 Johnny ___, "Key Largo" gangster
11 Bar bill
14 Circulation mainstay
15 Acquired relative
16 Yale Bowl rooter
17 Mistreated vegetable?
19 Zip
20 Make well
21 Choppers, so to speak
22 Mount Rushmore locale: Abbr.
23 Summer Games org.
25 Cupcake brand
27 Mistreated spice?
32 Author Rand
33 Castor or Pollux
34 A to E, musically speaking
37 Start over
39 Three, in a saying
42 Writer Ephron
43 Intimidate, with "out"
45 "Cold one"
47 Arles assent
48 Mistreated spread?
52 Wrinkly-skinned dog
54 In the past
55 Leprechaun's land
56 Select group
59 Words of woe
63 Speed limit abbr.
64 Mistreated meat?
66 Wall St. debut
67 Have a feeling
68 Jeweler's unit
69 Impresario Hurok
70 Coin words
71 Worshiped ones

DOWN

1 Price word
2 "Encore!"
3 Neck of the woods
4 Right-leaning?
5 Hasty escape
6 Tilt-A-Whirl, e.g.
7 Story starter
8 Dress
9 Drive-in server
10 Part of B.Y.O.B.
11 Greenhorn
12 Rap sheet handle
13 Swindles
18 "Yada, yada, yada . . ."
22 45-Across holder
24 Gives the go-ahead
26 Tanning lotion letters
27 Be a kvetch
28 Some whiskeys
29 Pop art icon
30 Patriotic women's org.
31 Space explorer
35 In alignment
36 Salon sweepings
38 Earthy pigment
40 Tie the knot
41 Discuss pros and cons
44 In fashion
46 Toupee, slangily
49 Bird with a showy mate
50 Pier's support
51 "What a shame"
52 They're weighed at weigh stations
53 Zoo heavyweight
57 ___ facto
58 Made tracks
60 Sizable sandwich
61 "Square" thing
62 New newts
64 Popular CBS drama
65 601, in old Rome

by Steven Kahn

ACROSS
1 List ender
5 Line crosser?
9 Brief argument
14 1984 Peace Nobelist
15 It might need two hands to be removed from a shelf
16 Work, in a way
17 "Topaz" author
18 Bearded bloom
19 Traffic sign
20 Flying an SST?
23 Pandora's boxful
24 Varnish ingredient
25 "Everyone welcome"
29 Kind of rule
30 Mattress problem
33 Bowser
34 What "that" ain't
35 Certain something
36 Missouri baby carriers?
40 French 101 verb
41 Before, before
42 Sight along the Mississippi
43 __-devil
44 See 13-Down
45 Comedians, e.g.
47 Icarus' undoing
48 Porkpie feature
49 Cost of a certain grain?
56 Sleep disturbance
57 1980's TV police comedy
58 Queens's __ Stadium
59 This puzzle's theme
60 Bit of roofing
61 Scuttle filler
62 Pope's writings
63 "No ifs, __ . . ."
64 Breaks off

DOWN
1 Place for pins
2 Go sour
3 Working away
4 W. C. Fields persona
5 Squelch
6 Marine deposits
7 Out of whack
8 First-place
9 1970's space station
10 Pioneering 1940's computer
11 Numerical suffix
12 Raconteur's offering
13 With 44-Across, handyman's task
21 Skater's figure
22 Artful dodges
25 Church areas
26 Far from eager
27 Nantes's river
28 Result of an oil surplus?
29 Part of spring in France
30 Urbane
31 Ordnance supplier
32 Some are inert
34 Cry's partner
35 Mars' counterpart
37 Sierra __
38 Eyeball
39 Roly-poly
44 Plantation libations
45 Noted traitor
46 Department store section
47 Take a powder
48 Niger neighbor
49 Bring to ruin
50 Knot
51 Loser to VHS
52 5K or 10K
53 "The heat __"
54 Part of a punch ballot
55 Some are shockers
56 Gullible one

by Ed Early

44

ACROSS
1 "Go, team!"
5 Good rate of speed
9 Skin
14 Atahualpa, for one
15 Eugene O'Neill's daughter
16 Blood line
17 Theater light
18 Sgts., e.g.
19 Peter and Paul
20 Rep's network
23 Waist, approximately
24 One leaving home, perhaps
27 Time mgrs.
28 Bear to look up to
31 Like a cloudless night
32 Not flat at all
34 River to the Ubangi
35 Kitchen set
40 Eclipse sight
41 "Citizen Kane" actor Everett ___
42 Entry
45 Thessaly peak
46 Calculating sort, for short?
49 Law enforcer since 1873
51 Crowns
53 Contractor's determination
56 Swing wildly
58 Where many Indians live
59 Purpose
60 Drink with a foamy top
61 Force ÷ acceleration
62 Send out
63 Doesn't ignore
64 Ignore
65 Words often listed together: Abbr.

DOWN
1 Returnee's question
2 Open, in a way
3 Comes down on
4 More than unpopular
5 Some of them have Handel bars
6 Nuts
7 A party to
8 Belt
9 Pol backer
10 It's hopeless
11 What smudges may indicate
12 Narrow connector: Abbr.
13 Is down with
21 Skulked
22 School media depts.
25 First name in mysteries
26 Blinkers
29 Tans
30 Certain Miamian
32 Cunning
33 They can be inflated
35 Apothecaries' weight
36 "___ Suave" (1991 hip-hop hit)
37 Sit on, maybe
38 Desperation, of a sort
39 Henry and June's friend, in a 1990 film
43 Station barriers
44 Part of R.S.V.P.
46 Smooth
47 Cram
48 Strong points
50 Wrapped cheeses
52 Areas connected to an ambulatory
54 Author Dinesen
55 Not final, as a legal decree
56 Old pop duo ___ & Eddie
57 Part of a science course

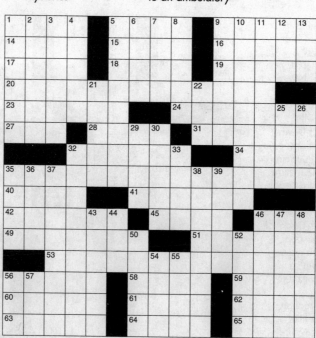

by Rich Norris

ACROSS

1 Ne plus ultra
5 He conversed with Wilbur
9 Classified information?
13 Corn __
14 Plow handle?
15 Soup vegetable
16 English poet laureate, 1692–1715
17 Royal burgh of Scotland
18 Rushes
19 They may run in the summer
22 Rooting parts
23 Popular snack cake
24 Dog-training aid
26 Shakes
30 Coastal Brazilian state
33 Unlike a typical hot dog
35 Title word of a song from Mozart's "Requiem"
36 Son of Haakon VII
37 They're left at sea
38 Magellan's grp.
39 Cartoon dog
40 Sorry soul
41 Jazz combo, maybe
42 100 centesimos, in Panama
44 Easily addled
46 Sell out, in a way
48 Daughter of King Pelles
52 Dickens character
56 Cut
57 Like some details
58 With 31-Down, "Sweet Liberty" star
59 "The Black Stallion" boy
60 Very long-winded answer

61 __ justes
62 Hebrew for "beginning"
63 Big game
64 It settles on sweeps

DOWN

1 Be for a bit
2 Staples, say
3 Taxi alternative
4 White House
5 Blend
6 One may draw blood
7 Verdi aria
8 Marsh birds vis-à-vis marshes
9 1808 resignee as U.S. senator
10 Depression era figure
11 Joel Chandler Harris title
12 Answer with attitude
14 Short on sharpness
20 __ vez (again): Sp.
21 Segar created her
25 Jesus on a diamond
27 "Shoot!"
28 Sufferer's desire
29 Candidate's goal
30 Schmo
31 See 58-Across
32 It comes down hard
34 Longfellow's bell town
37 Went on and on
41 Knesset : Jerusalem :: Storting : __
43 Propel, in a way
45 Lingerie shop purchase
47 Worth keeping, perhaps
49 White house?
50 "Marvy!"
51 Surrealism pioneer
52 Old crowned head
53 Radiance, of sorts
54 Some livestock
55 "Not true!"

by Michael Shteyman

46

ACROSS

1 Take out of the freezer
5 Whole lot
9 Nuclear weapon, in old headlines
14 Atmosphere
15 Fish in a salad
16 Confederate general, for short
17 Customer
18 Battery fluid
19 Momentary flash
20 "Pshaw!"
23 The Amish, e.g.
24 Spanish king
25 Show the effects of weight
28 Coffee container
31 "___ your age!"
34 Pick up the tab for
36 "In what way?"
37 Like rush hour traffic
38 "Pshaw!"
42 Gift on a first date, maybe
43 Can metal
44 Pilot light
45 She sheep
46 Kitchen set
49 End a fast
50 Cul-de-___
51 Warlike god
53 "Pshaw!"
61 Knock for ___
62 Sen. Bayh of Indiana
63 Lumber source
64 Wait on
65 Blend
66 Composer Stravinsky
67 Four-bagger
68 Whom a hunter hunts
69 Verne captain

DOWN

1 Tightly strung
2 "Pipe down!"
3 Vicinity
4 ___ and all (including faults)
5 Laundry stiffener
6 Transparent plastic
7 "National Velvet" author Bagnold
8 Dry riverbed
9 States one's case
10 "Button" site
11 Miscellany
12 Restaurant posting
13 "All ___ are off!"
21 Bench-clearing incident
22 Not leave enough room
25 Blank look
26 Cupid's projectile
27 Silly ones
29 German wine valley
30 Fashionable, in the 60's
31 Pound buildup
32 Pause indicator
33 Sound from a nest
35 Favorable vote
37 Weekend TV show, for short
39 City east of Syracuse
40 Family
41 #1 Beatles hit "___ Fine"
46 Certain piano pedal
47 Tex-Mex treat
48 Hip
50 Hotpoint appliance
52 Fine blouse material
53 Salt amount
54 Butter alternative
55 Typical amount
56 Dole's running mate, 1996
57 At any time
58 Press upon
59 Subj. with circles and such
60 Person with a medal, maybe

by Gregory E. Paul

ACROSS

1 Window base
5 One-tenth: Prefix
9 Within reach
14 Operatic solo
15 Dash
16 Children's song refrain
17 Al Capp parody of Dick Tracy
20 Octad plus one
21 Princely initials
22 On the sheltered side
23 Examines a passage
24 A prospector may stake one
26 Midwest hub
28 B westerns
33 Repair tears
36 MasterCard rival
38 Salman Rushdie's birthplace
39 User of air abrasion to clean teeth
43 Bewildered
44 Exam taken in H.S.
45 Pipe joint
46 African bloodsucker
48 It's given to a waiter
51 Breathing room
53 Reggae fan, often
57 Play divisions
61 Actor Wallach
62 Shoe part
63 Muscleman's garment
66 "Careless Hands" singer Mel
67 List-ending abbr.
68 Otherwise
69 Fess up
70 Wall St. trading center
71 Prognosticator

DOWN

1 Equipped with air bags, say
2 Castle of dance
3 Tropical vine
4 "Streets of ___" (cowboy song)
5 Exploit
6 Golfer Ernie
7 What credit cards may bring about, eventually
8 Prefix with structure
9 "For ___ a jolly . . ."
10 Verdi opera
11 Filmmaker Jordan
12 They show their faces in casinos
13 Oxen's harness
18 Whip
19 The Buckeye State
24 Like new dollar bills
25 Common street name
27 ___ Maria
29 Big blast maker
30 Make changes to
31 Soufflés do it
32 Glut
33 Squabble
34 Food, slangily
35 Sage
37 How a prank may be done, after "on"
40 Mosquito protection
41 Edinburgh girl
42 J.F.K. approximation
47 Sporting blade
49 Shore birds
50 Diaper wearers' woes
52 ___ wrench
54 Subway station device
55 To the point
56 More inclined
57 "The Thin Man" dog
58 Lump of dirt
59 Contract stipulation
60 Big rig
62 Castaway's home
64 One who looks Rover over
65 Swedish carrier

by Ed Early

48

ACROSS
1 Soda fountain purchases
6 Street fleet
10 Guest bed, maybe
14 Parting word
15 "We'll tak ___ o' kindness yet"
16 Iran is mem. of it
17 W
20 Publicity
21 When doubled, start of a cheer
22 "What foolishness!"
23 Rattrap
24 Valuable green stuff
25 Island near Corsica
27 X
34 Swedish exports
35 Strauss's "___ Rosenkavalier"
36 DVD menu option
37 Part of E.T.A.: Abbr.
38 What detectives follow
40 Sue Grafton's "___ for Evidence"
41 Turkish generals
43 Chronic misbehaver
44 Bag lunch eater?
46 Y
50 Sizable vessels
51 100-cent unit
52 Metro stop: Abbr.
55 Its hub is in Copenhagen
56 Actor Vigoda
57 At most, informally
60 Z
64 Violinist Leopold
65 "___ Brockovich"
66 Spoonful, say
67 Burro's cry
68 Wds. of similar meaning
69 Mr. Bean on the screen

DOWN
1 "___ help?"
2 God who rides an eight-legged horse
3 Gun's recoil
4 Cry of mock horror
5 Wide-brimmed chapeaux
6 Vacationer's vehicle
7 It isn't returned
8 Hit by strong winds
9 Sports car features
10 Blubber
11 Major work
12 Love or song ending
13 Like flu victims
18 White House staffer
19 Some Antietam combatants
24 Triangular sail
26 Piece of sound equipment
27 Esau's father
28 Florida's Key ___
29 Merlin Olsen, once, for short
30 Show flexibility
31 Wide-awake
32 Employee's request
33 Radio Hall of Fame inductee Kay
38 Chemical bonds
39 Go-between
42 Wee, to Burns
44 Opening of a toast
45 Lennon's love
47 ___ Minor
48 Pines
49 San Juan Hill site
52 One who crosses the line?
53 Promote an album, possibly
54 Sailing
57 Shoot past, e.g.
58 ___ saxophone
59 2000 sci-fi film
61 Test
62 Apéritif choice
63 "You'll go ___!"

by Alan J. Weiss

ACROSS

1 Camera setting
5 __ mai (dim sum dish)
8 Boston fish dish
13 Where a whale may be found?
14 Crush in competition
15 Relinquish
16 Dermatologist's concern
17 Saragossa's stream
18 Popular 1990's sitcom
19 Assistance from a tall librarian?
21 Ready to jump, perhaps
22 Bit of slander
23 Mensa administrations
25 Child actor?
29 Grogshop choice
30 H-dos-O?
31 "Holy cow!"
35 Paraphernalia
37 __-dog (Indian stray)
39 Welfare, with "the"
40 N.F.L. rusher Smith
43 Major show
46 Pasture
47 Husking bee refreshment?
50 Oleg Cassini had designs on her
53 Haunted house sound
54 Guide with a penlight
55 Ventriloquism?
60 City planner's concern
61 Prologue follower
62 Where Ibsen worked
63 Piece of gossip
64 Active ingredient in Off!
65 Puddle's cause, maybe
66 Closes in court
67 Put in
68 Sampler, of a sort

DOWN

1 Buck passers?
2 "This can't be good"
3 Grimm offering
4 End of a warning
5 Sleeps it off, maybe
6 Sling
7 Where nothing is wrong
8 One put away for the summer
9 It fingers ringers
10 Tees off
11 Manifest
12 Nicks' cousins
14 Moved, as art
20 Circus performer
24 Shopping channel
25 Like Solomon
26 Skelton's Kadiddlehopper
27 Kinko's unit
28 "Frida" star Salma __
32 City on the Rhein
33 A.C. or D.C., e.g.
34 "Awright!"
36 Threw caution to the wind
38 Let off the hook
41 Pines
42 Mardi Gras, e.g.: Abbr.
44 German toast
45 Brightly colored food fish
48 Fruity mixed drink
49 Countless
50 Case studier
51 Not separately
52 Paper ballot waste
56 Like some coffee
57 Listener's response
58 Shut (up)
59 Clown of renown

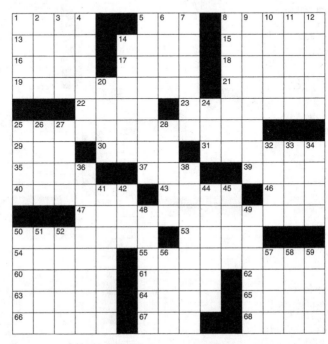

by Paula Gamache

50

ACROSS

1 "Hold on!"
9 Faultfinder
15 "No kidding!"
16 Labor organizer?
17 Learned
18 Set's victim, in myth
19 Takes a break en route
20 Start of some "regrets"
21 Roman well
22 Viagra and relatives, chemically
24 Les : French :: ___ : Italian
26 Brit's service discharge
27 Mean
31 Fashions
36 Was a cast member of
37 Northern air
38 "Bravo!"
39 Current principle
40 What something anomphalous lacks
42 Distance abbr.
43 Particle accelerator
47 Fly catchers
50 Instantly, after "in"
51 Ecaudate
55 Inveigh against
56 Meets
57 First king of England
58 Bill Clinton, e.g.
59 Fiddle finale?
60 Door openers

DOWN

1 Heir lines?
2 Home of ancient Chaldea
3 Minuscule
4 "___ tedious old fools!": Hamlet
5 Golden calf builder
6 Hold (off)
7 Cádiz compass point
8 Bully
9 Welder's tool
10 Sci-fi zapper
11 Livorno lady friend
12 "The Death of ___" (Jacques-Louis David painting)
13 Online publication
14 Observes the Sabbath
23 "That's O.K. with me"
24 Be beaverish
25 Like "la vida" in song
26 From the beginning
28 Snag
29 "Makes no difference"
30 Camel, e.g.
32 T or F: Abbr.
33 Dispense sound advice
34 City on the Ijsselmeer
35 They can go into the grain
41 Bag
43 Exposed
44 French story
45 Shaman's responsibility
46 Hurt
47 Flips one's lid?
48 "___ Dream" ("Lohengrin" piece)
49 Lose in a confrontation, maybe
52 That certain something
53 Command to Fido
54 Some young 'uns

by Manny Nosowsky

ACROSS

1 Games nobody wins
5 Small, medium or large
9 Green fruit drink flavor
13 West Coast gas brand
14 Shoelace problem
15 Get ___ a good thing
16 "Well, I'll be!"
19 Out for the evening, maybe
20 Gymnast Comaneci
21 Yogi or Smokey
23 Quart divs.
24 "Sesame Street" skills
28 Get-up-and-go
30 Folklore meanie
33 Overly, informally
35 ___-Cat (off-road vehicle)
37 Motor City labor org.
38 "If only . . ."
41 Late columnist Landers
42 Broadway hit letters
43 Cat that catches rodents
44 No longer on active duty: Abbr.
46 "Dumb" girl of old comics
48 Fourposters, e.g.
49 Got together
51 007
53 Photo tint
55 Port in "The Marines' Hymn"
60 "Stupid of me not to know"
62 Defeat decisively
63 Handle roughly
64 ___ gin fizz
65 ___-bitty

66 Stuff to the gills
67 Weigh station units

DOWN

1 Tex-Mex snack
2 Wrinkle remover
3 Quito's country: Abbr.
4 Auctioneer's closing word
5 Kid's wheels
6 Scared (of)
7 Animal house
8 English prep school
9 Deceived
10 Wearing a costume, say
11 N.Y.C. gallery
12 U-turn from WSW
17 Apply gently
18 Napkin's place
22 Greet the day

24 Battling
25 Daniel with a coonskin cap
26 "I don't want any part of it"
27 Cardinals' team letters
29 Dictatorship
31 Thumped fast, as the heart
32 Decorative jugs
34 Takes too much, briefly
36 Lennon's lady
39 Doofus
40 Kernel
45 Sheriff's sidekick
47 Cheap booze
50 Up to, informally
52 Fizzle out
53 Flu season protection
54 U.S.N. bigwigs
56 "Check this out!"

57 Norway's capital
58 "Exodus" author Uris
59 Fateful March day
60 ___ Lanka
61 Battery size

by Nancy Salomon and Harvey Estes

52

ACROSS
1 Was of the opinion
5 "Shake ___!"
9 Expensive wraps
13 Woodwind
14 Less welcoming
15 Straddling
16 Novelist Ambler
17 1970's-80's TV twosome
19 Recommended amount
20 Overseas Mrs.
21 Gerber offerings
22 Log holder
24 Syllables sung in place of unknown words
25 Winner
27 In the wrong
32 Pledge of Allegiance ender
33 Actor Bean
35 Androcles, e.g.
36 Fill the chambers, say
38 Arab League member
40 Put in storage
41 Company in 2002 headlines
43 Countrified
45 Barely maintain, with "out"
46 Mimics' work
48 Frequent ferry rider
50 "Kidnapped" author's inits.
51 Composer Boulanger
52 Black mark
56 Signal at Sotheby's
57 Steel mill by-product
60 1990's-2000's TV twosome
62 Coveted prize
63 Diva's delivery
64 Dust Bowl drifters
65 What Dubliners call home
66 Poverty
67 Jordan's Queen ___
68 Campus bigwig

DOWN
1 Worked in rows
2 Spain's second-longest river
3 1990's TV twosome
4 Iago's specialty
5 Hard nut to crack?
6 Money replaced by the euro
7 Rat alert?
8 Dads of dads
9 Evenhanded
10 Magazine of reprints
11 Took a cab
12 1974 Sutherland/Gould film
14 #1 hit for Brenda Lee
18 Imperatives
23 Outback hopper
24 ___ notes
25 Jacket holder
26 Massey of old movies
27 Personification of mockery
28 Oerter and Unser
29 1980's TV twosome
30 Elicit
31 Having a higher model number, say
34 Feudal laborers
37 John ___
39 Water nymphs
42 Silent film star Mabel
44 It was dropped in the 60's
47 Wine holder
49 Didn't speak clearly
51 More polite
52 E. B. White's "The Trumpet of the ___"
53 Goodyear product
54 Tennis great Nastase
55 Delighted
56 Scott of "Happy Days"
58 A celebrity may have one
59 Feds
61 "King Kong" studio

by D. J. DeChristopher

ACROSS
1 Broad comedy
6 H.S. math
9 Steinbeck family
14 Legend automaker
15 "Ben-___"
16 Dogpatch fellow
17 Wanted poster info
18 Drink in a mug
19 Botox targets
20 Chess endings that don't hold up?
23 Ad-___ committee
24 Rice Krispies sound
25 It makes pot potent: Abbr.
28 Ultimate degree
30 Look over, informally
35 Clarinet, for one
37 Brain-wave test: Abbr.
39 First name at the 1976 Olympics
40 Zombie calculation?
44 Resell illegally
45 Sign of summer
46 Numbskull
47 Sonora shawls
50 Granola morsel
52 European carrier
53 Yalies
55 ___ Cruces
57 Poisoned saltine?
63 Unclogged
64 Heston was its pres.
65 Imam's study
67 Waste maker, proverbially
68 Shrew
69 Singer Cleo or Frankie
70 Said "I'm in," in effect
71 Make like
72 Spanish hero

DOWN
1 Airways-regulating org.
2 Rights grp.
3 Undo
4 Wall Street debacle
5 Singer Sheena
6 Pequod skipper
7 Quiet times
8 Lorne or Graham
9 Pungent pepper
10 The last word
11 Green Gables girl
12 Stinky grades
13 Grads-to-be: Abbr.
21 Took steps
22 Kentucky Derby time
25 Bridge strengthener
26 "It follows that . . ."
27 Chest wood
29 H.R.H. part
31 Singer's backup
32 Baja "bye"
33 Supergirl's alias ___ Lee
34 Port east of Porto-Novo
36 Boxer Oscar ___ Hoya
38 Salon goo
41 Popped up
42 Corp. biggie
43 Australian "bear"
48 Polar helper
49 Reddish brown
51 Guard's neighbor
54 Deep-six
56 Swede's "Cheers!"
57 ___ Bator
58 Egg holder
59 More than fill
60 Frenzy
61 Idle in comedy
62 Indian princess
63 Chinese tea
66 Composer Rorem

by Jay Livingston

54

ACROSS

1 Subject of an Andrew Wyeth portrait series
6 Legacy
14 Duties
15 Slightly twisted
16 Isn't just theoretical
17 Tanning vats for reptile hides?
18 Apple computer delivery vehicles?
20 Service
21 Harvester ___
22 Word with rabbit or roasting
23 1939 Glen Gray hit "___ Night"
26 Word on a Ouija board
27 Gray, in a way
28 Like many resort areas
31 Woes of an itchy, twitchy dog?
33 Some game equipment
36 Floor protector
37 Coffee choice
38 Attack dog owner's remark to a burglar?
43 Guaranteed
44 TV cartoon dog
45 "Wham!"
48 Rare trick-taker
49 Assumed part of a Web address
50 Zenith competitor
51 Actress Gardner
53 Dental X-rays?
55 One who's brought in when shipments are damaged?
59 Unwell
60 Calligrapher's purchase
61 Compounds found in wine

62 Totals
63 Analyzes

DOWN

1 Hydrocarbon in petroleum
2 Sends off letters?
3 Shopper's aid
4 Words after "Oh, come on"
5 Salve
6 Hardly sophisticates
7 Muffs
8 Little bounder
9 Business abbr.
10 Extra amount
11 Folkie's choice of guitar
12 Gangster weapons
13 If not
14 Curtis ___, 1960's Air Force chief of staff

19 Roundly beat
23 Great deal
24 "We've been ___!"
25 Ending with ego or ideal
28 Aim to please
29 Big name in hardware
30 It's taken for a trip
31 Leg part
32 "Casablanca" role
33 Textile company purchase
34 Saturn model
35 Desserts eaten with spoons
39 It may follow you
40 Hotelier's handout
41 Frontier person
42 Working synchronously
45 Indulged in vanity

46 Becomes apparent (to)
47 Nasties in nests
49 Equine ankles
51 Another name for 30-Down
52 Windmill blade
53 Player's trophy
54 ___ bread
56 "Move it!"
57 Lifeboat item
58 God, in Italy

by Patrick Berry

ACROSS

1 Acceptance as cool, to some
11 Nuclear physics prefix
15 Pop choice
16 Examination room sounds
17 City on the Mahoning
18 Georgia and others, once: Abbr.
19 None too soon
20 Royal borough of Greater London
22 Nail-biting sports events, briefly
24 Knuckle-headed gestures of affection?
25 Lost it
30 Subject, usually
31 "I'll speak a prophecy __ go": Shak.
32 Headstrong one
34 Failed to
37 By and by
38 They're not too sharp
40 Level
41 Memorable sidekick
43 1999 Ron Howard film
44 Saab model
45 Base of a crocus stem
47 Daubs
49 University of Cincinnati player
52 LAX abbr.
53 Irrationality
55 "Gil Blas" writer
60 Cartoonist Walker
61 Base for some jellies
63 Paranoiac's worry
64 Gives freshman introduction, say
65 1974 Peace Nobelist Eisaku __
66 Lie

DOWN

1 __ bean
2 Certain harness race
3 Outfielder Mondesi
4 Sicilian resort
5 Pushes
6 Synthetic
7 Chi hrs.
8 Corner piece
9 Astronomer Hubble
10 Yoplait alternative
11 Fender, perhaps
12 Java locale
13 Pang
14 Leagues: Abbr.
21 Yummy
23 Bonehead
25 Nathanael who wrote "Miss Lonelyhearts"
26 Suffix with smash
27 Crayola color introduced in 1990
28 Painter whose name means "little dyer"
29 Bobs, say
33 "I'd like to give it a try"
35 Role in Racine's "Britannicus"
36 Suffix with 11-Across
39 Joseph Stalin's daughter
42 Quint's boat in "Jaws"
46 Animal on the field, perhaps
48 Aces
49 Some dermatological anomalies
50 Name on a famous B-29
51 1998 World Series winning manager
54 Hit hard
56 Row
57 Kind of recorder
58 Will of "Jeremiah Johnson"
59 Swedish actress Persson
62 __ and the Dragon (Apocryphal book)

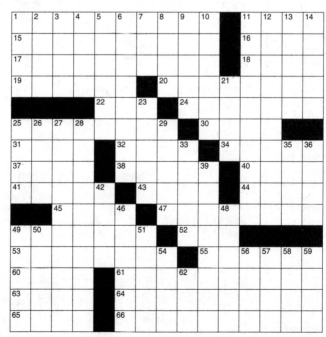

by Myles Callum

56

ACROSS

1 Gladiators' locale
6 Eskimo's vehicle
10 Office message
14 Snouted animal
15 "___ Get a Witness" (Marvin Gaye hit)
16 Sandler of "Big Daddy"
17 In reserve
18 Dashiell Hammett dog
19 Andes capital
20 Best available
23 ___-mo
24 Campaign (for)
25 Philosopher ___-tzu
28 Music, ballet, sculpture, etc.
31 Liquid part of blood
36 Shade trees
38 Trot or canter
40 Not for the first time
41 Quick, easy motion
44 Old silo missile
45 Pond duck
46 Countertenor's counterpart
47 Lackey
49 Men-only affair
51 Thesaurus listing: Abbr.
52 Whisper sweet nothings
54 Toy with a string
56 Where punches are hardest
65 Opera set in ancient Egypt
66 Greek promenade
67 Word before circle or tube
68 "Roger, ___ and out"
69 Hosp. printouts
70 Gawk (at)
71 County center
72 Attention-getting sound
73 More than dislikes

DOWN

1 Above
2 Punjabi princess
3 "Ben-Hur," for one
4 Shaving mishaps
5 Space on a leaf
6 "Begone!"
7 Eyelid attachment
8 Computer key
9 Telephone
10 Drink with a foamy head
11 Work for Hearst, e.g.
12 Hit musical with the song "Bosom Buddies"
13 Gen. Bradley
21 Do without
22 Acquired relative
25 Southpaw
26 "Kate & ___"
27 Leaves out
29 Roly-poly president
30 Locations
32 Home of the Taj Mahal
33 Explores the seven seas
34 Like some eyes at a wedding
35 Playwright Chekhov
37 Pyramid scheme, e.g.
39 "___ does it!"
42 Special skill
43 Tickle pink
48 Hangmen's ropes
50 Cry in a kids' card game
53 A lot
55 Ship of Columbus
56 New Mexico town on the Santa Fe Trail
57 Busy place
58 Brainstorm
59 Golfing vehicle
60 Robe for Caesar
61 Trunk fastener
62 Picnic pest
63 "From ___ to Eternity"
64 Uno y dos

by Randall J. Hartman

ACROSS

1 Use a swizzle stick
5 Sarcophagus
9 Skater Henie
14 Humanitarian org.
15 Track shape
16 Goodbye to José
17 Birthstone for many Libras
18 Personal staff member
19 Massaged places
20 Super
23 Ally
24 Versailles habitant
25 Married madrileña: Abbr.
28 Natural hairstyle
31 Disney's dwarfs, e.g.
33 Thick slice
37 Score of 100-0, say
39 Letter from a teacher
40 Treat with chips
43 Five-note refrain
44 Start of Caesar's last gasp
45 "Witness" director Peter
46 Doesn't contain one's anger
48 "Note to ___ . . ."
50 Stroke
51 Part of WWW
53 West of Nashville
58 Condition of utmost perfection
61 Capital near Casablanca
64 Cupid's Greek counterpart
65 Qatari leader
66 Dumbfound
67 Big name in auto parts
68 Sport in which players wear masks
69 "Unsafe at Any Speed" author
70 No short story
71 Orderly

DOWN

1 Jeer
2 Piglike animal
3 Farsi speaker
4 Confederate signature
5 How pendulums swing
6 "Metamorphoses" author
7 Volunteer org. launched in 1980
8 Cloudiness
9 Lindbergh Field site
10 Jazz singer Anita
11 Small bite
12 Friday on TV
13 Simpleton
21 Santa ___, Calif.
22 Classical Japanese drama
25 Investment
26 Diameter halves
27 "Doe, ___ . . ."
29 Lecher
30 Removes from power
32 Ship's front
33 Exorbitant
34 Longest river in France
35 Alaskan native
36 Spot on the radar
38 Head in a guillotine?
41 Big trouble
42 Dead-end street
47 Sun. delivery
49 Combatant
52 Geoffrey of fashion
54 Birdcage sound
55 Adagio and allegro
56 "But you promised!" retort
57 Tito Puente's nickname
58 Discomfit
59 Duffer's obstacle
60 Arizona tribe
61 Oversaw
62 Famous jour. publisher
63 One-star

by Adam Cohen

ACROSS

1 Jerry ___, mustachioed comedian with 8-Across
8 Late, great entertainer
15 Circuit well-trod by 8-Across
16 Liqueur flavoring
17 House Speaker nicknamed "Mr. Sam"
18 Job for a speech coach
19 Mideast bigwigs of old
20 Drinks daintily
22 Madeleine Albright's bailiwick, once
23 One of the 13 colonies: Abbr.
24 Oktoberfest serving
25 "Quiet, please!"
26 15-Across audiences
27 Swift avian
29 Faulkner character ___ Varner
33 Answer to "Are too!"
36 With 40-Across, 8-Across's signature song
38 8-Across film of 1940
40 See 36-Across
41 Kentucky Derby prize
42 Bygone U.S. gas brand
43 Elvis hit "A Fool Such ___"
44 CPR user, often
45 Early Dungeons & Dragons co.
47 Vincent Lopez's theme song
49 Morse bit
52 Speed: Prefix
55 Not fer
56 Poker?
57 Connived
59 Compared (to)
61 More than worried
62 Where 8-Across was born
63 Jane who co-starred in three 8-Across films
64 1933 Broadway musical that featured 8-Across

DOWN

1 Band-Aid rival
2 Inedible orange
3 True-blue
4 Wagering places, for short
5 ___-Turn (sign)
6 Some hospital staff
7 Golfer Palmer, to friends
8 Blackfish or redeye
9 Make a choice
10 Brief encounter
11 Satisfied, as a meal
12 Prefix with -gon
13 Laureate figure, maybe
14 Raison d'___
21 Staffing up early
24 "You're welcome, Hans!"
25 Warbled
26 Some bringers of baby gifts
28 ___ a time
30 ETs' ships
31 Age-old tales
32 Ancient Athens's Temple of ___
33 Museo holdings
34 Kind of scale
35 Scottish denials
36 General ___ chicken (Chinese menu item)
37 Destiny
39 Actor Epps
44 Pacific phenomenon
46 French river in W.W. I news
48 Gulf vessel
49 Gulf money
50 Regarding
51 Gossipy Hopper
52 Bygone autocrat
53 Rights grp.
54 Cartoonist Addams
55 Supplementary: Abbr.
56 Prefix with photo
58 Sushi fish
60 Former Vladimir Putin org.

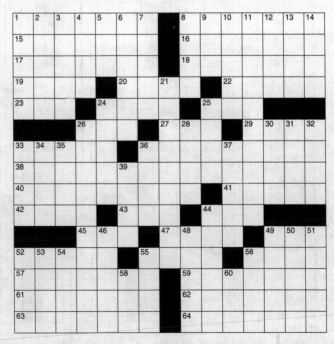

by Charles E. Gersch

ACROSS

1 Duck with a large white crest
5 Atkins diet count, briefly
10 Gillette product
14 ___ Alto
15 "I Could Write ___" (Rodgers and Hart song)
16 Jacob who wrote "How the Other Half Lives"
17 Not be childish
19 Private dining room?
20 Greek island or its capital
21 Wraps (up)
23 Prussian pronoun
24 Burn preventer
25 Neighborhood shindig
27 Folders, wastebaskets and such
29 Adriatic seaport
30 No longer young
31 "Forever Your Girl" hitmaker, 1989
34 It may get you slapped
38 Very, affectedly
39 Literal element of eight answers in this puzzle
40 Arrange, as hair
41 Cheerleader's maneuver
43 1974 title role for Dustin Hoffman
44 October 31 option
45 Super server
47 Revolution
48 For sale
50 Line of defense
53 Old-time marauder
54 Timber wolf
56 Orangish hues
58 Wild goings-on
60 Becomes discouraged
62 Stamp of approval?
63 Mower maker
64 Top spot
65 Train station
66 City near Oberhausen
67 Sweetie

DOWN

1 Knocks heads (with)
2 ___ Picchu (Incan site)
3 John with a wild wardrobe
4 Percussion instrument struck with a mallet
5 Olive oil dressing
6 ___ of Steel (video classic)
7 Swelter
8 One over
9 Twist
10 It may be twisted
11 Paints the town red
12 Symbol of Japan
13 Burden carriers
18 Sherpa's land
22 Charlie Brown utterance
26 Winchester, e.g.
28 Basic building unit
29 Huge success
30 "Shoot!"
31 Flight coordinators: Abbr.
32 It may be on a roll
33 Heroic action
35 Unnamed litigant
36 Showy display
37 Bug someone, e.g.
39 All-natural food no-no
42 Rampart
43 Hanger-on
46 Elect
47 G's
48 They're found among the reeds
49 What counters may count
50 "It's ___ against time"
51 Skin layer
52 Aromatic compound
55 Part of many an antique shop name
57 Nincompoop
59 Chatter
61 It comes before long

by Greg Staples

60

ACROSS
1 Medium for some social protest
9 Eritrea's capital
15 Unanimously
16 Unwise thing to run from
17 Talent scout's request
18 Pick democratically
19 Like some trade
20 Wears
21 Pear type
22 It may be fenced
23 Strong stuff
26 Pal of Potsie and the Fonz
30 "___ She Coo?" (#1 R & B hit for the Ohio Players)
31 Supersize order
35 Carbonium, e.g.
36 What clones share
37 Association
38 Mustangs, e.g.
40 Sun-cracked
41 "Scooby-Doo" girl
42 One of three Ottoman sultans
43 Fabled fliers
45 Korda of tennis
47 One of a bunch
49 Blasts
53 New Jersey city
54 Two-time U.S. Open winner
55 Most impressive
56 Charlie is in its ads
57 Florida's ___ Key
58 Taxes

DOWN
1 In things
2 Hebrew prophet in the Douay Bible
3 Broad-topped hill, in the Southwest
4 Like many a door
5 Introduce robots, say
6 Panama's Torrijos Herrera and others
7 Quaker Oats brand
8 Hit below the belt, in a way
9 Rugged transportation, for short
10 Be bad with goods?
11 Copycat
12 New Olds of 1999
13 "Something to Talk About" singer
14 Bristlelike appendages
23 Go down a lane, maybe
24 Grand
25 A dog's age
27 Stammerer's words
28 Follow-up series to "See It Now"
29 Garden store stock
31 Rugged transportation
32 Squib, say
33 Douglas Hyde's land
34 Open position?
36 Public policy initiated in the 1980's
39 Jewel boxes
40 Fun house features
42 Habit
43 Geometry calculations
44 In abeyance
46 Old flask heaters
47 Uncle ___
48 Stage org.
49 The Bee Gees' "___ Liar"
50 "Within ___ a hell": Shak.
51 Choice word
52 Ocean crossers

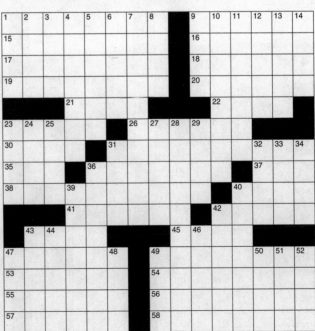

by Jim Page

ACROSS

1 Help in crime
5 Hard baseball throws
9 1983 Woody Allen title role
14 Foot: Prefix
15 Do desk work at a newspaper
16 "Don't Cry for Me, Argentina" musical
17 Old math calculating tool
19 747 flier
20 Mischievous
21 Attention-getter in an ad
23 Mystery writer Dorothy
25 Kind of sauce
26 Get rid of
29 ___ clef
34 When a plane is due in: Abbr.
37 Odd souvenir
39 Defect
40 Baseball . . . with a hint to this puzzle's theme
44 Mishmash
45 African-American
46 Duffer's goal
47 Blind dates, e.g.
50 Hibernation
52 Locale for Switz. or the U.K.
54 Creek
58 Top 40 song list
64 Welsh dog
65 Early computer
66 Barn tool
68 Sassy
69 Get ___ shape
70 ___ fixe (obsession)
71 Irritable
72 Campus bigwig
73 Golf ball props

DOWN

1 Church recesses
2 Abzug of the National Women's Hall of Fame
3 Instruct
4 Cleaned (up)
5 The "p" in m.p.g.
6 Instruction: Abbr.
7 ___ monster
8 "Let it stand" orders
9 Gentle breeze
10 Devil's work
11 "___ Marlene" (classic song)
12 "Try ___ for size"
13 Garden entrance
18 Physicist Fermi
22 Place for a nap
24 Shock
27 Ill-tempered one
28 Rome has seven
30 Eastern newt
31 Radar image
32 Buddhist monk
33 Pitcher, but not the diamond kind
34 1940's-50's All-Star ___ Slaughter
35 Narrative
36 Going ___ tooth and nail
38 Milky gem
41 Paper in lieu of payment
42 They're worth 1 or 11 in blackjack
43 Outline
48 "Splendid!"
49 Big ___, Calif.
51 Business motive
53 Swift
55 Eat away at
56 Be in accord
57 Studio sound equipment
58 Weight
59 Concerning, to a memo writer
60 Neckwear
61 History, with "the"
62 Eat fancily
63 Kett of old comics
67 Jailbird

by Ed Early

62

ACROSS

1 Have ___ on one's shoulder
6 Sumptuous
10 At a distance
14 Sprocket projections
15 Ready to eat
16 Dear, to Donizetti
17 Muse of poetry
18 Hipbones
19 Red "Sesame Street" character
20 39-Across component
23 Denver clock setting: Abbr.
24 Suffix with social
25 Drive-thru bank feature, for short
26 Baby carrier?
29 Some beach toys
31 Question for a brown cow?
33 Early baby word
36 Place
38 Two-time U.S. Open winner Fraser
39 Way to fitness
42 Reluctant
43 Shorebird
44 Radiation measures
45 In the unique case that
47 Common mistakes, say
49 Concorde
50 Form of ID: Abbr.
52 Wish undone
53 Flapper accessory
56 39-Across component
60 Iota
62 1997 Peter Fonda role
63 Milk: Prefix
64 "And ___ bed"
65 Baseballers Guidry and Swoboda

66 Old-fashioned theater
67 Name of more than 20 popes
68 Scared sounds
69 Diaper, in Britain

DOWN

1 Special Forces unit
2 Asteroid first sighted in 1801
3 It's strengthened by 20-Across
4 "Tell ___ the judge"
5 You may have one for spiders
6 Sales brochure feature
7 Perfume ingredients
8 Star in Virgo
9 It can be improved by 39-Across
10 Air force heroes
11 Alias
12 Offshoot
13 Milne marsupial
21 Formal reply to "Who's there?"
22 Surrounded by
27 Automaton
28 Actress Verdon and others
29 Socialists, e.g.
30 Knight's need
32 River dams
33 Site of an oracle of Apollo
34 Certain transmitters
35 Took care of
37 Perfect
40 Texas cook-off dish
41 Boredom
46 It can be improved by 39-Across

48 Pan films?
51 Ravel's "Daphnis et ___"
53 It's strengthened by 56-Across
54 Leading
55 Intense suffering
57 Harrow rival
58 Lengthy footrace
59 "And here it is!"
60 Dow Jones paper, for short
61 ___-ha

by Karen M. Tracey

63

ACROSS

1 Biblical gift bearers
5 Kuwaiti, e.g.
9 You can say that again
14 Lena of "Chocolat"
15 Rake feature
16 Fasten, as a ship's rope
17 Vendor's vehicle
18 Clock sweeper
19 Stupefy
20 Significant events outside the U.S.?
23 One of the Sinatras
24 High dudgeon
25 Oust
28 Oral surgeon's deg.
29 Tête-à-tête
33 Egg: Prefix
34 Hornswoggled
36 Reproductive body
37 Some caterpillars outside the U.S.?
40 Work with the hands
41 Actress Zellweger
42 Service for eight, e.g.
43 Charon crosses it
44 Neighbor of Leb.
45 Grasping
47 Microwave
48 One with her own dressing room, surely
49 With "the," everything outside the U.S.?
57 Kachina doll makers
58 Beat fast
59 Swing around
60 At attention
61 Berkshire school
62 __ group (computer info source)
63 Amusingly eccentric
64 "Cut it out!"
65 Flippant

DOWN

1 Poke fun at
2 Jai __
3 Song on the Beatles' "Rubber Soul" album
4 Altogether
5 Literary institution: Var.
6 Vaquero's rope
7 British royal
8 Laid up
9 Taper off
10 Audition tape
11 Broadway's __ Jay Lerner
12 Look (at)
13 Looks at
21 Handled badly
22 Alums-to-be: Abbr.
25 Loading areas
26 Olympic category
27 Full of firs
28 Dissuade
29 Minor U.S.N. administrator
30 One taken for a ride
31 Equipped with a heater?
32 Snappish
35 Formed beads, in a way
36 Turn suddenly
38 Purchase price addition
39 Infantry unit
44 Hunter of old movies
46 Gobbles
47 Piquant
48 Radioactivity cleanup process, for short
49 "I'm glad that's over!"
50 Kibbutz dance
51 Grp. with barrels
52 Spank
53 Defense acronym
54 In addition
55 One with second thoughts, say
56 Muralist José María

by Mel Taub

ACROSS

1 E.R. amts.
4 Geographical name that means roughly "great land"
10 "An Essay on Criticism" essayist
14 Leftover bit
15 Reading of 98.6°, e.g.
16 Casual footwear
17 First-rate
18 Singles' world
20 Pre-Red head
22 Tiny complaints
23 Oklahoma tribe
24 Moving
26 Tries
28 Lap dog
30 Kind of radio
34 Alphabet trio
37 Stalled construction
38 For some time
40 Peter Cottontail's pace
42 Ella Fitzgerald classic
43 Station rating
44 Speaker in the outfield
45 Shropshire female
46 Some Joe Frazier wins
47 Irons
50 Drang's partner
51 Yellow parts
55 Cause for a blessing?
59 Hike
61 A millionth of a milli-
62 Nickel-nursers
65 Not go straight
66 Rabble
67 Phone button
68 Hosp. readout
69 Cards traded for Musials, maybe
70 Burly
71 Blue hue

DOWN

1 White vestment
2 Traverse back and forth
3 Annual parade honoree, briefly
4 Clause joiner
5 Museum deal
6 Craftsmanship
7 Lovestruck
8 Part of the Louisiana Purchase
9 H.S. subj.
10 Sgt.'s charges
11 Olive genus
12 Rec room activity
13 It involves a wave of the hand
19 Terse radio message
21 Basket feature
25 Six-Day War figure
27 "Out!"
29 Trendy
30 Spa sounds
31 Stand-up's prop
32 Zoomed
33 Parcel (out)
34 Kerflooey
35 Pendulum accompaniment
36 Capable of
39 Spineless
41 ___ de deux
42 Perfumed
44 House mover?
48 Old arm
49 Roughly one of every two deliveries
50 Pacifier
52 Lolls
53 Trinket
54 Damp
55 Prefix with phobia
56 Small talk
57 Importance
58 Galoots
60 Scaler's goal
63 Yearbook sect.
64 Wily

Note: Twelve answers in this puzzle are to be entered in an unusual way, for you to discover.

by Patrick Merrell

ACROSS
1 Vets
8 Suits
15 Like some apartments
16 Recommended safety limit
17 Crumbly
18 Swelling reducers
19 Amender
20 Free
21 Items on a 46-Down, perhaps
22 Big name in outdoor grills
24 Word interpreted by Daniel
25 Getty Center architect Richard
27 Blazer, e.g.
28 Transplanted, as a plant
29 "Unsung, the noblest deed will die" poet
31 Buffoonery
33 Knocks the socks off
35 Not regular
39 Swabber
44 Grable's "The Dolly Sisters" co-star
45 Where to find porters
47 Writer Alexander
48 "And Morning __ with haste her lids": Emerson
49 Like some number systems
51 Bavarian river
52 Sink
54 Go back
56 Controlled
57 Osgood Hall Law School locale
58 By and large
59 Thus spake Zarathustra

60 Lifts, in a way
61 What Alfred E. Neuman has

DOWN
1 Many an exit
2 Rock singer?
3 Like some restaurants
4 Beat the drum for
5 Side in gray
6 Set to keep warm, perhaps
7 Metric measures
8 Earliest
9 Old Renault
10 Origin of man
11 Nutritive matter around a seed's embryo
12 Closely connected
13 Fan sites
14 Some stanzas
23 Barbershop request

26 Shower shower?
28 Slopes
30 Cooler than cool
32 Ad catchword
34 Numbers of places
35 Recovered from a bad stroke?
36 New arrival on a reservation
37 Have in common with
38 Don't hold your breath
40 1979 film loosely based on Janis Joplin's life
41 Shade close to plum
42 Very poor, in a way
43 Service aces?
46 A round may be added to it
49 Newbery-winning writer Scott

50 John X's successor
53 Land in S.A.
55 Norman with a club

by Sherry O. Blackard

66

ACROSS

1 Plaster work
7 Icy
11 Jacuzzi
14 Pay a visit to
15 Hawaiian cookout
16 What an assessor assesses
17 Meeting all requirements
19 Inventor Whitney
20 Christmas trees
21 Ahead of schedule
22 Backs of the thighs
23 Subject of an S.E.C. inquiry
25 Go out with
26 Heel
27 Unlikely Planned Parenthood member
32 Precedes
35 Lower the grade of
36 Former White House spokesman Fleischer
37 "___ only me"
38 Pay-___-view
39 Mrs., in Madrid
40 Babe
42 Monastery or convent
44 Not planned
46 Aussie hopper
47 Bit of sunshine
48 Expensive fur
52 Computer in-box annoyance
54 Prison-related
56 Café au ___
57 Santa's subordinate
58 Unpretentious
60 Whistle-blower?
61 Away from the wind
62 Cantankerous
63 Undergrad degs.

64 Holler
65 Far-flying seabird

DOWN

1 Leave a mark on, as shoes
2 Snouted Latin American animal
3 Ne plus ___
4 Finality
5 Firms: Abbr.
6 A while back
7 Bordeaux and others
8 Factory store
9 Delicate
10 Forehead-slapper's cry
11 Loyal
12 Body part that's sometimes "greased"
13 Line of symmetry
18 Spates

22 Barber's focus
24 Investigate
26 White-collar workers?
28 Annoyed, eventually
29 Cinema house name
30 Raison d'___
31 Derrière
32 Go bankrupt
33 19th-century writer Sarah ___ Jewett
34 Disreputable groups
38 Dabble in
41 Speck
42 TV selection
43 Leak stopper
45 Embroidery yarn
49 Less decorated
50 Petrol measure
51 Antiknock compound

52 Belgrade native
53 Not guilty by reason of insanity, e.g.
54 Vaulter's tool
55 Orbit
58 Calendar unit
59 Prior to, to Prior

by Craig Kasper

ACROSS

1 Cows and sows
5 Coarse file
9 Four-alarmer, e.g.
14 Lt.'s superior
15 "Dies ___"
16 Raring to go
17 To boot
18 Muses count
19 Wield, as influence
20 Get angry, as a mechanic?
23 Buck's mate
24 Mother of Dionysus
25 "Do the Right Thing" pizzeria
27 City near Provo
30 Play time
34 Houston athlete
38 Bakery buy
40 "Garfield" dog
41 Get angry, as a bicyclist?
44 Wholly absorbed
45 Like hen's teeth
46 Jennifer of "Flashdance"
47 "The Lion in Winter" star
49 Actress Lanchester
51 Make over
53 When mastodons disappeared
58 Grp. with students' interests at heart
61 Get angry, as a missile designer?
64 Arrival at a refinery
66 Estrada of "CHiPs"
67 Bumping one's head on the ceiling, say
68 Impolite look
69 A few
70 First name in scat
71 Yankees manager Joe
72 50's British P.M. Anthony
73 Take a load off

DOWN

1 Strike breakers
2 Oscar-winning Berry
3 English racing town
4 "Uncle Tom's Cabin" author
5 Horseshoes score
6 It might hit the high notes
7 ___ souci
8 Sneaks a look
9 Popular VW
10 Left Coast airport letters
11 Old
12 Round number?
13 Old Harper's Bazaar artist
21 Distant
22 You're on it
26 Serving with tea
28 Suffix with oper-
29 Olympic skier Phil
31 Early Icelandic literature
32 Place to dust
33 Matches, as a wager
34 Big do
35 Bed support
36 Keyboard slip
37 Turbine part
39 Walk like a sot
42 A Corleone son
43 Old adders
48 4-Down's Simon
50 Smooth and soft
52 Beyond pudgy
54 Fragrant substance
55 Dickens title opener
56 Breathers?
57 Brilliance
58 Drop in the mail
59 Former Yugoslav leader
60 Winged
62 Noted A.L. third baseman, for short
63 Drink garnish
65 Blow it

by Richard Hughes

68

ACROSS
1 ___ whisker
4 Jazz (up)
9 City across the Missouri from Council Bluffs
14 Balderdash
15 Bean seen on TV
16 Wizardry
17 XXX counterpart
18 Pay for, with "of"
20 Electrical units
22 Sweet wine
23 Having some success
25 Crown ___
29 Church party
30 Keep ___ (persevere)
32 Jeans name
33 Woven strands
35 "Oh, sure!"
36 Bodies making their closest approach in more than 50,000 years on August 27, 2003
41 Users of electrolocation
42 Shredded
43 G.P. grp.
44 Reasons
46 Takes off
50 Surroundings
52 Waldenbooks competitor
53 Parade chief's rank
56 With 63-Across, where the Kings play in Sacramento
57 Remove uncertainty
61 Fair-hiring inits.
62 Fab Four member
63 See 56-Across
64 Hill dweller
65 Bygone
66 Fence alternative
67 Opener

DOWN
1 Worries
2 "Anyone home?" call
3 Kind of number or weight
4 Crying out loud?
5 Canine neighbor
6 "Forever Blue" singer Chris
7 Field reporter: Abbr.
8 Tolkien's ___ of Fangorn
9 Breakfast order
10 Big parrot
11 Back, in time
12 The guy's
13 Pretense
19 Muslim pilgrim
21 Shoots from cover
24 Celebration
26 Italian island
27 Look like a creep
28 Places for props
30 A Musketeer
31 Leader before Lenin
34 ___-bitty
35 Old family Chevy
36 Lions or Tigers
37 Half in front?
38 Israeli airline
39 Teasing
40 ___ mater (brain membrane)
44 Irritate
45 Smart
47 When it's blue, it's fast
48 Epoch when mammals arose
49 Nose-in-the-air
51 Picture
52 Bleated
54 Onetime throne occupier
55 This spot
57 ___-Magnon
58 "___ Abner"
59 Swan song
60 "Norma ___"

Note: 18- & 22-Across and 53- & 57-Across have a hidden connection to 36-Across.

by Manny Nosowsky

ACROSS

1 Collar
4 "___ Said" (Neil Diamond hit)
8 On the job
14 Go off
15 Kind of dance
16 Dormmate, affectionately
17 Start of an idle question
19 Household
20 Understood
21 Mumbo jumbo
23 Exit
26 Keel-billed bird
27 Part 2 of the quip
33 ___ Bay, off Long Beach, Calif.
37 Superman's baby name
38 Purple shade
39 Spelling of TV
42 "Me neither"
43 "Let's give ___!"
45 Completely
47 Part 3 of the quip
50 ___ Lingus
51 Coffee bar treats
56 Shrinks
61 City known for its cheese
62 Gets working, in a way
63 End of the quip
66 Madison, for one
67 Not yet final, as a decree
68 Lacrosse contingent
69 Some Singaporeans
70 Carrier to the Mideast
71 Saucer contents, for short

DOWN

1 Salamanders
2 Buddhist who's attained Nirvana
3 Utah's ___ Canyon
4 Chemist's study
5 Draft pick
6 Bell and others
7 Apple that may be green or red
8 One with designs on others
9 Part of a skater's shoe
10 Habit
11 Epps of "Higher Learning"
12 Latvia's capital
13 Stay fresh
18 Quick swim
22 ___-di-dah
24 Food stamp

25 Banks on the runway
28 Greek vacation spot
29 Tennis ace Mandlikova
30 Very much
31 Florida's ___ Beach
32 1558–1603 monarch: Abbr.
33 Rain, but just barely
34 Wheels
35 Final Four org.
36 Coatroom features
40 "Carmina Burana" composer
41 American-born Jordanian queen
44 Good fellow
46 Spring Playgirl magazine V.I.P.
48 Green lights
49 Table scrap

52 Part of a balance
53 Blabber
54 Ant, in dialect
55 Composer Camille Saint-___
56 Garden party?
57 St. Petersburg's river
58 Old union leader I. W. ___
59 1960's Soviet moon program
60 Holiday song word
64 Texas tea
65 "The Good Old ___" (song classic)

by Elizabeth C. Gorski

ACROSS

1 Goddard of "Modern Times"
9 Really succeed
14 Spots
15 "Buenos Aires" musical
16 Ravi Shankar was part of it
17 Prediction tool
18 Evil
19 Kind of lepton
20 Tongues may cover them
22 Did farmwork
24 Injures
25 Flap
26 Hägar the Horrible's daughter
27 Not just any
30 Both, at the start
33 Pumped up, in a way
35 Subjects, say
37 Junho to junho, e.g.
38 Lightly brand
39 Getting something in the eye?
41 One going off to college, maybe
42 East ender?
43 Out of the oven, say
44 Show ___
46 Ring bearer?
48 "Thou canst not then be false to ___": Polonius
52 New York City bridge, informally
54 Cigarette holder: Abbr.
55 Cooler
56 Fair collection
57 St. Lawrence Seaway port of entry
60 Hal Foster's Queen of the Misty Isles
61 Redistributed
62 Like some divorces
63 Airport worker

DOWN

1 Philadelphia suburb
2 On ___ (hot)
3 Teutonic connector
4 On the Big Board
5 Nueva York, por ejemplo
6 Big chunk of moola
7 Case studier, slangily
8 One mushed
9 What a waiter or a track bettor does
10 Like a violet leaf
11 Rubber giant
12 Crowning
13 Dumpsite sights
14 Needle
21 A perfect square
23 "Mule Train" singer, 1949
24 Actress Doherty
28 Extremely popular
29 Early home
30 Requirement for some games
31 "Jerry Maguire" actor Jay
32 Relative of muttonchops
33 Arteries
34 Posh
36 "Unfortunately . . ."
40 Saturnine
44 General effort?
45 There from the start
47 Supports, in a way
49 Dye obtained from aniline
50 Contemporary of Freud
51 Future preceder
52 Public transportation
53 Stir up
54 Variety of trout
58 Flash
59 It's good in Paris

by Gilbert H. Ludwig

ACROSS

1 "Moby-Dick" captain
5 Excellent, in modern slang
9 Speedy
14 Greek sandwich
15 Poland's Walesa
16 Actress Verdugo
17 1998 Sarah McLachlan hit
18 Bullets, e.g.
19 Like lettuce or spinach
20 Considerable sum of money
23 Trigonometry abbr.
24 Soften
25 Barnyard honker
27 Apprehension
30 "Make it ___!" ("Hurry!")
33 Dadaism founder
36 Overrun
38 Venus de ___
39 Get schooling
41 "___ Fine Day" (1963 Chiffons hit)
42 Satisfy a debt
43 Just twiddling the thumbs
44 Recorded
46 Musician Brian
47 Red addition to a salad
49 Bring out
51 L'Enfant ___, in Washington, D.C.
53 Knights' weapons
57 Gift offered with an "aloha"
59 Useful tip for puzzle-solving?
62 Variety of primrose
64 Struggle for air
65 1997 Peter Fonda title role
66 Part of a bicycle wheel
67 ___ fruit (large tangelo)
68 Walking difficulty
69 Lugged
70 Espied
71 "Airplane!" actor Robert

DOWN

1 Open-mouthed
2 Nine-headed serpent
3 Sign after Pisces
4 Sailed
5 Toddlers' enclosure
6 Rope material
7 Pinnacle
8 Revealing beachwear
9 Use for support
10 Ginger ___
11 Something smoked at an Indian ceremony
12 Data
13 Word with "Happy" and "Death Valley" in old TV titles
21 Shroud of ___
22 Winning margin, sometimes
26 Identical
28 English river
29 "Inferno" writer
31 Blueprint
32 Toy that does tricks
33 Touched down
34 Make over
35 Handheld computing device
37 Wanted-poster option
40 Honest-to-goodness
42 Summary
44 Move like molasses
45 Gun part
48 Bugged
50 "Stop right there!"
52 Cattle breed
54 Paramecium propellers
55 Foe
56 Dance components
57 Needing directions, say
58 Montreal ballplayer
60 Parrot's spot
61 ___ of Man
63 1950's White House nickname

by Barry Silk

ACROSS

1 Swiftly
6 Leading the pack
11 Programming problem
14 "M*A*S*H" clerk
15 Hawaiian hello
16 William Tell's canton
17 Subject of a parable of Jesus
19 New IBM hire, maybe
20 ___ Victor
21 Play for a sap
22 Bridge
23 Take off the books
26 Squandered
28 Major work
29 "___ had it!"
31 Rich tapestry
32 A sib
33 Tankard filler
34 Set of principles
36 Conniving sort
38 ABC or XYZ
41 Serving on a spit
42 Bar bill
43 Comedian Olsen
44 Greet the day
46 Run smoothly
47 Level on the evolutionary ladder
48 Produce, as heat
51 Villain's epithet
53 Nile cobras
54 Long-jawed fish
55 Black cuckoo
56 Two liters, e.g.: Abbr.
57 Lewis Carroll poem
62 Big time
63 Encyclopedia section
64 Actor Milo
65 Sloppy digs
66 Barn dances
67 Whinny

DOWN

1 Artist Jean
2 Something to try to shoot
3 Fuss
4 Core groups
5 Novelist Jong
6 J.F.K. overseer
7 Shed light on
8 Martini's partner
9 Pumps and clogs
10 Beachgoer's goal
11 Farm abundances
12 University of Illinois locale
13 Mel Ott's team
18 Telescope pioneer
22 Bit of mistletoe
23 Katharine of "The Graduate"
24 DeMille production, e.g.
25 "Boris Godunov," for one
27 Sir, in old India
30 "Make" or "break"
33 Honey-colored
34 Ides rebuke
35 Mine transport
37 Lets up
39 Away from the wind
40 Leathernecks' lunch
44 Century plants
45 Vacation spot
46 Like some tea
47 Melodious
49 Playing marble
50 Put off, as a motion
52 Not achieved
57 Shake up
58 Pothook shape
59 Sorority letter
60 Fraternity party staple
61 Derisive cry

by Ed Early

73

ACROSS

1 Ruin, as hopes
5 See 53-Down
9 Precise
14 Actor Morales
15 "The Art of Love" poet
16 Like "Goosebumps" tales
17 Flounder's filter
18 After 41-Across, a religious set
20 Nutrition author Davis
22 You might stick a knife in it
23 Clue gatherer: Abbr.
24 College term
26 Something found around the house
28 Game show announcer Johnny
30 Within a holler
34 Carnival buy
37 Little Oz visitor
39 Big name in locks
40 "Did you ___ that?"
41 Theme of this puzzle
42 Like webs
43 "___ and Janis" (comic strip)
44 The paradise of "Paradise Lost"
45 Map markings
46 Vagabond
48 "The Millionairess" actress
50 Unvarying
52 Backslide
56 ___-cone
59 City west of Tulsa
61 "Harvey" role ___ P. Dowd
62 After 41-Across, a vaudeville set
65 Libido
66 Jittery
67 Loyal
68 Diminutive suffix
69 Mortar user
70 Thanksgiving dish
71 Germany reunifier

DOWN

1 "Dancer Lacing Her Shoe" artist
2 "Oh, by the way" comment
3 Door-to-door work
4 After 41-Across, a geographical set
5 Barrel race venues
6 "___ fallen and . . . !"
7 Florence farewell
8 To everyone's surprise
9 Pooh's gloomy pal
10 Crosses (out)
11 Needing irrigation
12 Motion picture
13 Try out
19 Use for support
21 Easter ___
25 Eminent
27 After 41-Across, a calendar set
29 "Lord Jim" or "Lucky Jim"
31 Spellbound
32 Like a robin's egg
33 Cravings
34 "___ she blows!"
35 Dynamic opening?
36 Famous White House pooch
38 Pavarotti, e.g.
41 Tranquil
45 Order to a broker
47 One of the Waughs
49 ___ Pieces
51 Neat
53 With 5-Across, a Caribbean island, formerly
54 Reality, old-style
55 Short-lived Ford
56 Big bridge win
57 Actress Foch
58 Baseball's Ed and Mel
60 "___ the Explorer" (kids' show)
63 General on Chinese menus
64 Dessert reaction

by Myles Callum

ACROSS

1 Babushka
6 Dot-___
10 Tel ___
14 Nasty and then some
15 Knee-slapper
16 Home to some Sargents, with "the"
17 Fabled fall guy
19 Biol. branch
20 "___ lazy river . . ." (Bobby Darin lyric)
21 Shoe decoration
22 Wheat variety
23 Loafer, e.g.
25 Kind of a drag
27 Dehydrated
28 1926 hit "Sleepy Time ___"
31 Hardly peppy
34 Indian beads
36 Short and thick
37 Ground cover
40 Slow outflow
43 "Ulalume" poet
44 Two of ten
46 One in a black suit
48 Birdbrains
50 Sports officials
51 Airy melody
55 Composer Bruckner
57 Element in some batteries
59 Let have
61 Eastern Canadian Indian
64 Run up a phone bill
65 Homecoming attendees
66 It's a wrap
68 "On & On" singer Erykah ___
69 Orchid products
70 Not smooth
71 Batter's bane

72 "___ She Lovely" (Stevie Wonder song)
73 Knots

DOWN

1 Downhiller's run
2 Ball up
3 Domestic
4 Emeritus: Abbr.
5 Jet off for
6 Buds
7 Klutz's cry
8 Sacred song
9 Doctor's lance
10 Was humiliated
11 Big sucker
12 ". . . like ___ not!"
13 Soft palate
18 "I'll be a son of a gun"
24 Backed bench
26 Gave pills to
29 Make like

30 Kind of payment
32 Nasdaq debut, maybe: Abbr.
33 Food additive
35 Holding
37 Benchmark: Abbr.
38 "So that's it!"
39 "Dragnet" signature sound
41 "Killer" PC program
42 Shell holder?
45 Studies
47 The past, in the past
49 Kenyan's neighbor
52 "No more, thanks"
53 Network (with)
54 Spills
56 Frasier's brother
58 Shrewdness
59 Street fleet

60 Ben-Gurion is its hub
62 Chili powder ingredient
63 Niagara Falls feature
67 Not to

by Nancy Salomon and Bob Peoples

ACROSS

1 "Alas"
5 Berated
15 Catch but good
16 Bouncer's place
17 Frumpy
18 Bad bit
   of planning
19 Title heroine
   of 1816
20 Bullets
21 "Concentrate!"
22 Baked dish
23 Media attention
24 Turns aside
25 Here
27 Cooler
29 Piccolomini
   Library's home
30 Unreason
31 As shown, for
   short
34 "Beats me"
37 Part of a swap?
38 Whom Scarpia
   double-crosses
39 Midwest city
   abutting Eden
   Prairie
40 "Cherish those
   hearts that ___
   thee": Shak.
41 Behind bars
42 Chihuahua, e.g.
46 Boomer or buster
47 Some Texas
   A & M degs.
48 Thoreau's
   "___ on the
   Concord and
   Merrimack Rivers"
49 Sheepish look
51 Kodak or Fuji
   competitor
52 Start of
   a conformist's
   phrase
54 Marshal Kane's
   time
55 Tots
56 Wrong

57 Flout the
   pecking order?
58 Mythology
   anthology

DOWN

1 Banked
2 Blues player,
   maybe
3 American Airlines
   Arena team
4 Portoferraio's
   island
5 Hair piece?
6 Lie, slangily
7 Pace
8 911 responders:
   Abbr.
9 Knuckle dragger
10 Landlord's
   entitlement
11 Yale name
12 Slew
13 Concerning

14 Ship woods
23 Like hawks
24 Titan's place
26 Common girl's
   middle name
27 Brothers
   on the air
28 Radio code word
30 Certain protest
31 Deserving at
   least a B
32 Another name
   for Tennessee
33 Start of a request
35 Rocket
36 Old leftist grp.
41 Quality of being
   fashionable
42 Two-masters
43 In the least
44 Quarterback
   Rodney
45 Numerical
   prefix

46 Something
   New York and
   Los Angeles
   each have
49 Understand
50 Rice-A-___
51 Chip in
53 Cultural org.

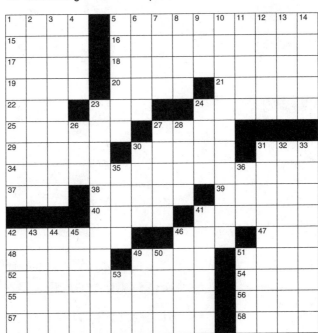

by Manny Nosowsky

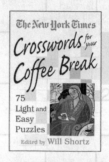
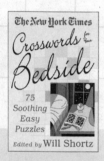

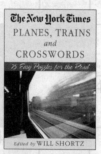

Crossword Puzzles

1

S	A	N	G	■	R	A	V	E	■	H	E	M	E	N
C	L	I	O	■	E	D	E	N	■	A	L	I	C	E
R	O	C	K	■	F	O	R	T	H	R	I	G	H	T
A	H	E	A	D	■	■	N	E	E	D	■	S	O	S
M	A	R	R	I	A	G	E	R	I	T	E	■	■	■
■	■	■	T	E	A	R	■	■	R	O	A	M	E	D
A	I	R	S	T	R	I	P	S	■	P	R	O	X	Y
I	R	E	■	■	P	E	L	T	S	■	P	I	E	■
L	A	N	D	S	■	G	O	A	L	P	O	S	T	S
S	N	O	O	T	S	■	■	R	E	A	R	■	■	■
■	■	W	I	L	B	U	R	W	R	I	G	H	T	■
O	A	R	■	L	O	O	N	■	■	E	E	R	I	E
G	H	O	S	T	W	R	I	T	E	■	N	E	L	L
R	E	V	U	E	■	E	T	A	L	■	T	A	L	E
E	M	E	N	D	■	S	E	R	F	■	S	T	Y	X

2

M	A	P	S	■	T	A	D	A	■	F	I	F	T	Y
A	L	O	P	■	A	T	O	M	■	I	N	U	S	E
G	A	P	E	■	N	E	W	Y	O	R	K	S	P	A
I	M	P	L	Y	■	I	S	S	U	E	■	S	S	R
C	O	A	L	M	I	N	E	■	N	T	H	■	■	■
■	■	■	S	A	D	■	■	A	C	R	E	A	G	E
A	R	C	■	■	S	T	A	T	E	A	B	B	R	S
R	O	R	E	M	■	A	D	O	■	P	E	R	O	T
T	W	O	L	E	T	T	E	R	S	■	■	A	W	E
S	E	C	E	D	E	S	■	■	A	R	A	■	■	■
■	■	■	C	A	P	■	L	A	N	D	D	E	A	L
E	S	C	■	L	I	L	A	C	■	S	A	M	O	A
F	L	O	R	I	D	A	K	I	N	■	G	O	R	Y
F	O	C	U	S	■	M	E	D	E	■	E	T	T	E
S	T	A	R	T	■	E	R	S	E	■	S	E	A	R

3

J	A	D	E	■	S	O	D	A	S	■	L	A	V	A
A	L	U	M	■	I	P	A	N	A	■	O	T	I	S
C	O	T	T	A	G	E	I	N	D	U	S	T	R	Y
K	E	Y	■	I	N	N	S	■	B	E	I	G	E	■
■	■	■	A	M	A	T	■	A	G	O	■	C	O	T
B	U	N	G	A	L	O	W	B	I	L	L	■	■	■
A	S	E	A	T	■	■	A	I	R	T	I	G	H	T
L	E	A	R	■	T	A	X	E	D	■	Q	U	A	I
E	S	T	I	M	A	T	E	■	■	A	U	T	R	E
■	■	■	C	A	B	I	N	C	R	U	I	S	E	R
F	A	A	■	R	U	T	■	L	O	R	D	■	■	■
A	L	B	E	N	■	■	L	A	M	A	■	C	O	S
L	O	D	G	E	A	C	O	M	P	L	A	I	N	T
S	N	U	G	■	C	A	N	O	E	■	D	A	T	E
E	E	L	Y	■	T	B	I	R	D	■	Z	O	O	M

4

T	H	E	■	G	E	T	M	E	■	S	O	A	P
A	O	L	■	U	N	W	E	D	■	F	E	S	T	A
C	L	E	■	I	S	I	T	I	■	I	N	C	A	N
H	A	V	E	T	U	X	■	T	A	N	T	A	R	A
■	■	■	P	A	R	T	I	■	R	E	T	R	I	M
B	Y	W	I	R	E	■	N	E	E	S	O	N	■	■
L	A	I	C	■	■	A	P	L	U	S	■	I	N	G
A	L	L	■	B	O	B	H	O	P	E	■	G	E	O
B	E	L	■	A	S	I	A	N	■	■	A	H	A	B
■	■	T	O	R	I	E	S	■	P	A	L	T	R	Y
B	E	R	A	T	E	■	E	L	E	N	A	■	■	■
E	L	A	T	E	R	S	■	U	S	O	S	H	O	W
E	L	V	E	R	■	W	A	G	E	R	■	O	L	A
B	I	E	R	S	■	A	L	E	T	A	■	P	I	C
E	E	L	S	■	■	B	A	R	A	K	■	I	O	O

5

C	A	M	U	S	■	P	I	C	A	■	I	N	C	A
O	V	E	R	A	■	O	N	U	S	■	B	A	L	E
B	A	L	I	N	■	W	A	R	H	A	M	M	E	R
B	L	O	C	K	L	E	T	T	E	R	■	E	V	A
L	O	T	H	A	I	R	■	I	N	T	■	S	E	T
E	N	T	■	■	P	A	W	N	■	B	L	A	R	E
■	■	■	G	U	I	D	O	■	C	O	O	K	E	D
■	T	H	U	N	D	E	R	S	H	O	W	E	R	■
S	H	O	A	T	S	■	S	T	A	K	E	■	■	■
L	E	M	M	A	■	S	T	O	P	■	■	S	I	P
O	N	E	■	C	O	Q	■	C	E	Z	A	N	N	E
S	E	P	■	K	N	U	C	K	L	E	B	O	N	E
H	E	A	D	S	T	A	R	T	■	V	O	C	A	L
E	D	G	E	■	O	R	E	O	■	O	V	A	T	E
D	Y	E	S	■	P	E	E	N	■	N	O	T	E	D

6

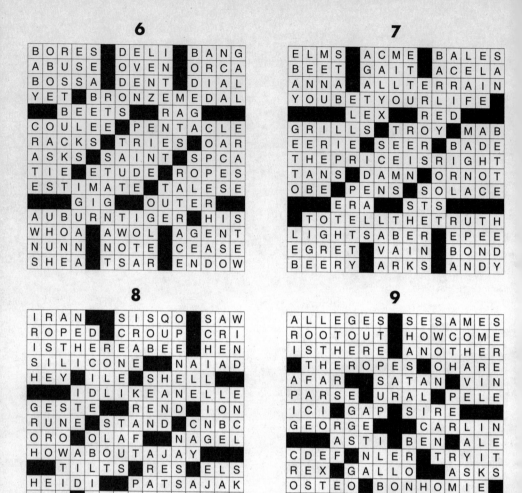

7

8

9

10

11

```
G R A P E ■ L A S T S ■ W A N
A T L A S ■ E S T E E ■ A B E
B E A T T H E H E A T ■ L B S
■ ■ T A U ■ E A S T ■ K I T
L E T I T B E ■ D E L E T E S
A N A ■ E R A S ■ S E T H ■
I N K ■ S I G H S ■ S T E M S
R U E D ■ S L A T E ■ U T A H
S I T U P ■ E L A N D ■ A R A
■ H O R S ■ L I M E ■ L I D
P R E S O A K ■ D E B A K E Y
L I C ■ F L I P ■ S E T ■
O N A ■ F I L L T H E B I L L
T S K ■ E N L A I ■ R A D I O
Z O E ■ R E S T S ■ S T O U T
```

12

```
F I R ■ I T S M E ■ K I C K
A M A T ■ G O T O N ■ E T O N
U P T O N O G O O D ■ L A M E
N A T T E R S O N ■ I L L B E
A L L O W ■ ■ P E N N Y ■
S E E ■ A F T ■ D O T ■ C O P
■ ■ I D I O M ■ T H R O N E
C O U L D N T B E B E T T E R
C A M E R A ■ A N A M E ■
S R S ■ E L M ■ O D O ■ S H E
■ ■ A S S A M ■ N A T A L
B L O T S ■ N O I S E L E S S
R O U E ■ S U N D A Y B E S T
E C R U ■ O A T E N ■ A R L O
W I S P ■ B L E A K ■ S E N
```

13

```
B A B E S ■ S C U D S ■ R I D
A Q U A S ■ T O M E I ■ I S R
J U S T W H A T W A S ■ P L Y
A I D E ■ A R T ■ D I P P E R
■ E R S T ■ A A H ■ A L T O
E A P ■ T H E G R E A T E S T
L D O P A ■ R E C A N T ■
M A T I L D A ■ A T T I M E S
■ C A E S A R ■ H E E L S
T H I N G B E F O R E ■ N I T
H E M I ■ A R R ■ U M P S ■
I P E C A C ■ I R E ■ A W L S
R C A ■ S L I C E D B R E A D
D A S ■ T E N A M ■ O S A K A
S T Y ■ A S S N S ■ D E R E K
```

14

```
I N T E R ■ S E C T ■ I O N ■
S A B L E ■ A T O N ■ M R E D
R E S E W ■ C H A T ■ M A T E
■ M A O R I S ■ P U L S E
I N T E R S E C T I O N ■
M O U N D S ■ A L E U T S
P I N T S ■ C O I N S ■ N E A
A S I S ■ P O U N D ■ S H E S
L E N ■ N O M S G ■ F A U N S
E D G I E R ■ C A R R I E
■ C O N C E N T R A T E D
D O Z E N ■ A B O R T S ■
I T E M ■ D I S H ■ H O N O R
M I R E ■ O N E I ■ E T U D E
■ C O N ■ C E N T ■ R A T E D
```

15

```
G I J O E S ■ B O O M M I K E
E N E S C O ■ U N B I A S E D
T H E M O U N T A I N K I N G
A U R A ■ R O T ■ S I E N N A
G M E N ■ P H E W ■ S A T Y R
R A D ■ G U I D E R ■ C O G S
I N A C A S T ■ T O G A ■
P E T A L S ■ G O L F E D
■ S L E W ■ T E E L I N E
D O N S ■ S I Z E R S ■ O T C
A R E A S ■ G L E E ■ A R A L
S I G N A L ■ O T B ■ L E I A
H E A D F O R T H E H I L L S
E N T R E A T Y ■ R U B L E S
S T E A R N E S ■ T R I O D E
```

16

H	E	D	D	A		T	R	E	E	D		C	S	T
A	L	A	I	N		H	E	N	C	E		R	E	B
J	O	I	N	T	H	E	C	L	U	B		U	R	I
	S	T	O	O	L			R	I	S	E	R		
E	L	Y		N	E	I	L	D	I	A	M	O	N	D
S	O	M	E		S	P	O	O	N		P	E	A	S
C	L	A	S	S		O	S	C	A	R				
	L	E	T	S	M	A	K	E	A	D	E	A	L	
		R	E	A	R	S			A	S	I	A	N	
S	P	C	A		S	C	E	N	T		S	R	T	A
W	I	L	D	A	T	H	E	A	R	T		H	E	P
O	N	E	A	L			M	O	O	S	E			
R	N	A		G	A	R	D	E	N	S	P	A	D	E
D	E	N		E	M	A	I	L		C	A	D	E	T
S	D	S		R	A	N	G	Y		A	T	S	E	A

17

	A	H	A	B		V	A	S	T		I	B	I	D
A	G	O	G	O		A	M	O	R		N	O	S	E
G	O	O	E	Y		P	T	U	I		B	L	E	W
A	R	E		O	U	I	S		P	H	O	O	E	Y
L	A	Y	A	B	E	D		B	L	U	R			
			T	O	Y		G	R	E	E	N	T	E	A
D	E	W	E	Y		B	L	A	T	S		A	N	T
O	B	O	E		L	O	U	I	S		S	P	O	T
E	A	R		W	O	O	E	D		C	H	E	W	Y
S	Y	M	P	H	O	N	Y		S	H	E			
			R	E	N	E		D	U	E	L	L	E	D
S	C	R	E	W	Y		B	O	I	L		O	V	A
U	L	E	E		B	U	O	Y		S	O	O	E	Y
E	V	A	N		I	D	O	L		E	R	I	N	S
Y	I	P	S		N	O	P	E		A	B	E	T	

Sixteen answers in this puzzle rhyme: GOOEY, PTUI, DEWEY, CHEWY, LOUIS, SUEY, BUOY, etc.

18

D	E	L	T	A		M	I	F	F		R	A	M	P
E	Q	U	U	S		O	R	E	O		E	G	A	L
B	U	G	L	E		I	M	A	X		G	O	T	O
T	I	E	S		F	L	A	S	H	L	I	G	H	T
S	P	R	A	W	L			T	O	S	S			
			R	O	O	T		L	U	T	H	E	R	
P	E	R	R	Y	W	H	I	T	E		R	I	D	E
A	L	O	E		I	T	E		A	L	G	A		
G	A	T	E		C	O	L	E	P	O	R	T	E	R
E	L	I	X	I	R		E	M	I	L				
		A	D	A	R		L	A	B	E	L	S		
F	A	R	M	A	N	I	M	A	L		A	L	A	W
E	L	O	I		K	N	I	T		A	N	I	S	E
U	P	O	N		U	S	E	R		A	C	H	E	D
D	O	M	E		P	E	N	A		H	O	U	S	E

19

	T	E	N	U	R	E	D			D	E	N	G
N	I	N	E	T	Y	D	E	G		R	O	D	E	O
E	G	G	B	E	A	T	E	R		I	N	I	G	O
E	E	R					E	U	G	E	N	E	S	
D	R	O	P	I		L	I	E	S	H	E	A	V	Y
			S	I	N		S	C	A	N	T			
V	I	S	T	A		H	E	N		T	A	R	O	T
I	D	E	A	L		A	L	G		U	P	E	N	D
M	I	D	S	T		P	A	L		R	I	V	E	S
			I	L	E	N	E		N	A	E			
G	R	E	A	T	O	D	D	S		O	N	R	E	D
L	E	G	P	U	L	L					S	A	Y	
A	C	R	E	D		I	S	R	A	E	L	I	T	E
S	T	E	R	E		V	I	N	G	R	O	O	M	S
S	O	T	S			B	A	R	N	O	N	E		

20

S	H	O	O	F	L	Y	P	I	E		S	L	A	M
F	A	L	S	E	T	E	E	T	H		M	I	C	A
G	R	E	E	N	C	A	R	D	S		A	N	T	I
I	D	O		G	O	G	I			A	R	G	O	N
A	W	L	S		L	E	G	W	A	R	M	E	R	S
N	A	S	A	L		R	E	E	D	S		R	S	T
T	R	E	V	O	R		E	L	L	E	R			
S	E	N	E	C	A	S		L	I	N	E	A	G	E
			D	A	M	U	P		B	A	D	B	O	Y
A	S	S		L	I	L	A	S		L	I	S	L	E
G	E	T	R	E	S	U	L	T	S		D	E	F	S
H	E	R	O	S		M	A	I	L		N	C	O	
A	S	E	A		B	A	T	T	L	E	S	T	A	R
S	T	A	N		I	M	O	U	T	A	H	E	R	E
T	O	M	S		D	O	P	E	S	H	E	E	T	S

21

```
JIHAD ■ CSPAN ■ SST
ATARI ■ ALEUT ■ TWO
WATERTROUGH ■ AIR
■ ■ STORM ■ ETNA
SNL ■ GOODENOUGH
LAUGHAT ■ RAISES ■
ISLEY ■ PACT ■
THUMBINGTHROUGH
■ RHEA ■ ISSUE
CAVIAR ■ ESCHERS
BREADDOUGH ■ RUS
RENT ■ DRUID ■
ACE ■ GOLDENBOUGH
CHI ■ ARIES ■ INTRA
TED ■ PEERS ■ SEERS
```

22

```
CASH ■ CRASS ■ MAZE
ANTE ■ YECCH ■ OPEN
ROAM ■ ADORE ■ NENE
HITEANDWAITE ■
ONEND ■ PLAYPEN
PTS ■ DASH ■ ALBUMS
■ GENIES ■ ASIA
■ REEDANDWRIGHT
CART ■ ODIUMS ■
HIATUS ■ AGEE ■ EGG
ALSORAN ■ ACURA
■ KNIGHTANDDEY
ELAN ■ LAIRD ■ ROTE
LOCO ■ EIEIO ■ ORES
FLEW ■ DODOS ■ MALT
```

23

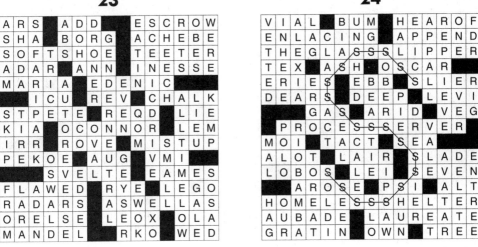

```
ARS ■ ADD ■ ESCROW
SHA ■ BORG ■ ACHEBE
SOFTSHOE ■ TEETER
ADAR ■ ANN ■ INESSE
MARIA ■ EDENIC ■
■ ICU ■ REV ■ CHALK
STPETE ■ REQD ■ LIE
KIA ■ OCONNOR ■ LEM
IRR ■ ROVE ■ MISTUP
PEKOE ■ AUG ■ VMI
■ SVELTE ■ EAMES
FLAWED ■ RYE ■ LEGO
RADARS ■ ASWELLAS
ORELSE ■ LEOX ■ OLA
MANDEL ■ RKO ■ WED
```

24

```
VIAL ■ BUM ■ HEAROF
ENLACING ■ APPEND
THEGLASSSLIPPER
TEX ■ ASH ■ OSCAR ■
ERIES ■ EBB ■ SLIER
DEARS ■ DEEP ■ LEVI
■ GAS ■ ARID ■ VEG
■ PROCESSSERVER ■
MOI ■ TACT ■ SEA ■
ALOT ■ LAIR ■ SLADE
LOBOS ■ LEI ■ SEVEN
■ AROSE ■ PSI ■ ALT
HOMELESSSHELTER
AUBADE ■ LAUREATE
GRATIN ■ OWN ■ TREE
```

25

```
DCCOMICS ■ SIMBAS
NEEDANAP ■ ENORME
ALLALONE ■ AGLEAM
LIL ■ TUNABLE ■ TRI
ACAN ■ TOKES ■ CHIS
BARES ■ NOL ■ MARLO
■ STUFFONESELF
WASTENOTWANTNOT
CLASPEDHANDS ■
FINIS ■ DEV ■ SOPUP
ITIN ■ CEDED ■ NONO
EAT ■ TOREROS ■ LVI
LLAMAS ■ VANHALEN
DIRECT ■ IGNOREIT
SAYSOS ■ LEADENLY
```

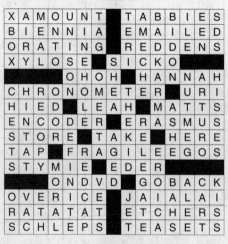

26

CHIC · CAVE · YIELD
HIDE · ARID · ERROR
EVEN · MANE · SALSA
FEATHERONESNEST
SARA · III
AAH · RATTLER · PTA
TRESS · ASI · SOON
LEATHERSTOCKING
ANDY · VAT · LINER
SAY · CAYENNE · TRY
SOD · EARS
HEATHERLOCKLEAR
AGREE · EACH · URSA
HALER · AROO · MIEN
ADORE · PANS · PEAK

27

EXPAT · JOVE · PTAS
MEESE · AHEM · LAME
INAWE · LARA · EXEC
LAKESHORECABIN
SHAPE · IRE
CAMPILY · BAT · BMT
ICIER · EAT · FAIR
VACATIONGETAWAY
ISAK · MTV · HILTS
LES · GAB · JEERSAT
DUG · FORAY
SEASIDECOTTAGE
PAWN · NERO · RADON
BRAT · EVAS · ILIAD
SANE · SOLE · CENTS

28

RAH · EMCEE · AGORA
INA · LIRAS · VIPER
STRAYDOGSHELTER
KIDS · CLEON · ISA
SIXTEENOUNCES
MOHAIR · TEA
ELI · VISTA · SCHMO
ALPS · POUND · LIEN
LASIK · ONTAP · TAU
RAF · ROMANS
MONEYINLONDON
ETO · ALOOF · NDAK
STRIKEWITHFORCE
TEASE · AREAL · UTE
ARDOR · YENTA · NIL

29

STEM · BIRDS · SHAQ
HEXA · ATARI · OAHU
ANTI · JONAS · LIAO
STANDARDBARER
TENSE · ISLE · LUG
ART · AMY · DUETO
GREENGROSSER
OTTO · LAYLA · ESPY
SHEEPSHEERER
SALSA · EEL · SPA
AWE · TRAM · SMART
CHEESEGREATER
OKAY · ASTRA · RIFE
WISP · PEREZ · AVES
LATE · STOWE · TART

30

XAMOUNT · TABBIES
BIENNIA · EMAILED
ORATING · REDDENS
XYLOSE · SICKO
OHOH · HANNAH
CHRONOMETER · URI
HIED · LEAH · MATTS
ENCODER · ERASMUS
STORE · TAKE · HERE
TAP · FRAGILEEGOS
STYMIE · EDER
ONDVD · GOBACK
OVERICE · JAIALAI
RATATAT · ETCHERS
SCHLEPS · TEASETS

31

```
C H O P . L E N S . S I F T S
A O N E . A L O U . I D I O T
P A I R . N E A L . L A R G E
G R O U N D C H U C K . E S T .
U S N . E M T . . A H A B . .
N E S T E A . . I N A R U S H
. . S T R A P S . T I G E R .
D A M E . K N E A D . S S T S
R O O T S . D A N U B E . . .
S L O S H E S . C E S S N A .
. . N E A R . A K A . A I R
B A R . T R U S T B U S T E R
A L O F T . S A R I . N I C E
E M C E E . E V I L . O R E S
R A K E R . D E A L . W E S T
```

32

```
N A A C P . E M M A . D O O R
O C C U R . M O A T . A N N E
T H R E E R I N G C I R C U S
E Y E . P O G O . H O N E S T
. . . F A I R . F I N . . .
J E R R Y L E W I S . L A M A
A L I A S . . I D O . A V I D
N O D S . F E L O N . B E A M
E P E E . A D M . . N O R M A
T E R R . D E A N M A R T I N
. . . P E N . E A T S . .
A N G O R A . M E N U . J A I
H O L L Y W O O D O R B U S T
O P E D . A L O E . A O R T A
Y E N S . Y A R D . L O Y A L
```

33

```
V A T . B A L M S . J E R K Y
I S R . A T E U P . U N T I E
C H A I N M A I L . I N E P T
T O U R D E F R A N C E . .
I R M A S . S O Y . I D S
M E A N . O U G H T . A C R E
. . N A N A . I N A B I T
. F I V E T I M E C H A M P
G O T H A M . E V E L .
T G I F . E A S E D . G I T S
E S C . P A T . M E N S A
. . Y E L L O W J E R S E Y
Q U E E N . A E R O S M I T H
B R O W N . S N A G S . S S E
S I S S Y . T O P S Y . T E Y
```

34

```
E Q U I N E . C A W . O R T
L U M M O X . O H B E . P E A
S E A F O X . F L A P J A C K
. . . N O D T O . T O Q U E
J A M S . N E H R U . G U R U
E Q U I P . W E I S S . E S P
D U L L E S . A D L I B . .
. A L L T H E L E T T E R S .
. . S T O M P . A U L A I T
W A V . Y E A H S . P I Z Z A
A V I V . S N A C K . E Z E R
F A C E T . A B H O R . .
F L U X G A T E . D A Y J O B
L O N . I G E T . A R E O L A
E N A . F E D . K E N Y A N
```

35

```
S L E E P S O F F . C A B A L
V O X P O P U L I . A L I C E
E S C A L A T E S . D E L T A
L E O . E S T A T E S . K I D
T I N T . M O P E Y . S E V E
E T S E Q . S I D E C H A I R
. . Q U I E T . F O U N T S
. I G U A N A . T U N N E Y
D R O I D S . M U L A N .
R O L L S O V E R . N E S T S
I N G A . L I A N A . D O R A
E M O . P E A S O U P . N I B
D I T T O . G L U T A M A T E
U N H I P . R E T R A C T O R
P E A C E . A S S Y R I A N S
```

36

```
R A P T   I L I A D   D A D A
I S L A   N A C R E   U S E D
C L A N   O N E O F A K I N D
H A N G I N G L O O S E
I N T O W     M R T   I D S
E T A   O C T O   M I L T I E
  T E N D E R S   A S A N
  F I T T I N G E N D I N G
A L O T   S A L E R N O
M O N E T S   N A D A   B I O
Y E S   R E S     F L I T S
  S I T T I N G T I G H T
B A B Y B O O M E R   E G A L
O M E N   F L A R E   N I C E
Z I N C   F E N D S   S E A R
```

37

```
B I B B   P I A F   O F O L D
O N E A   U G L I   R E N E E
M E L O N B A L L   Z E S T A
B R I B E S   T I T O   L I D
  T E A M   S O A K   E A T S
    B O U I L L O N C U B E
A D D S   M A D   P T A   R O G E T
C R O   S A M   P T A   H M O
T Y P O S   A A A   S T E N
I C E C R E A M C O N E
V E N T   S C A T   E E L S
I R A   G E T Z   R E S O L E
S E N S E   S O L I D F O O D
T A C I T   U N T O   I S P Y
S L E D S   P S S T   T E E S
```

38

```
A C R E S   P S S T   A M A N
S O U T H   A W A Y   L E N A
I N T H E B L I N K O F A N I
A S H O R E   N E E D   N I L
  S P A D E   D A T E S
B I D   A T E   S K I D
O D I E   P O L I T I C A L
H E R E S M U D I N Y O U R I
R E T R E A T E D   S E G O
  I N D Y   E R A   S O N
P A R E D   G R E C O
A D E   U S S R   E R U P T S
T H E A P P L E O F O N E S I
T O S S   R O T E   S C O O T
I C E S   Y E A R   S E N S E
```

39

```
J E E P   A N N E   S A D A T
O T T O   G O B Y   A B E L E
A T A[NY]P R I C E   B A[NY]A N
N U T T I E R   D O L O R S
  A L E   D A Y T O N
I N D I E   P I L L   N E A P
D E A L S   L O L A   E S S O
T A M   B U[NY]A N   E S P
A T O P   A S S N   S H L E P
G O N E   D E U S   L O F T Y
  R E C E S S   R O M
O C U L A R   D E M O T E S
C A[NY]O N   P R I S O[NY]A R D
T R O U T   L E O I   M Y N A
S A N T O   Y A R N   S E E K
```

40

```
M A D D O G   M O S T O F I T
A L E P P O   A U T O R A C E
N A S S E R   S T A R T R E K
I M P   R E J O I C E   M A W
T E A R   N I N N Y   S E G A
O D I U M   G I T   F A D E R
B A R B E R S C H A I R
A S S Y R I A   E N L A C E S
  D R A W T O A C L O S E
L A C E Y   P A P   H E N C E
O T O E   T U B E R   E S A S
N E E   R E Z O N E D   U L A
G A R B A N Z O   T A X L A W
E S C A R O L E   O D E T T E
D E E P E N E D   P A R S E D
```

41

S	M	A	C	K		S	H	E	D		S	H	O	P
P	U	R	E	E		P	E	T	E		M	O	M	A
A	S	T	O	R		A	L	U	M		O	P	E	N
T	H	E	S	C	O	R	P	I	O	N	K	I	N	G
			H	E	E		T	O	Y					
O	R	C	H	I	D		C	A	I	N		J	F	K
R	E	L	E	E		H	A	L	O		T	E	L	E
T	H	E	A	F	R	I	C	A	N	Q	U	E	E	N
H	A	F	T		E	L	H	I		U	N	P	E	N
O	B	S		D	A	L	E		Y	E	A	S	T	Y
		S	E	C		H	I	E						
T	H	E	L	I	T	T	L	E	P	R	I	N	C	E
H	U	L	A		I	R	A	S		E	V	I	A	N
I	S	I	S		N	E	W	S		S	O	C	K	O
S	H	A	H		G	E	N	E		T	R	E	Y	S

42

E	M	A	I	L		R	O	C	C	O		T	A	B
A	O	R	T	A		I	N	L	A	W		E	L	I
C	R	E	A	M	E	D	C	O	R	N		N	I	L
H	E	A	L		T	E	E	T	H		S	D	A	K
		I	O	C			H	O	S	T	E	S	S	
C	R	A	C	K	E	D	P	E	P	P	E	R		
A	Y	N		S	T	A	R			F	I	F	T	H
R	E	D	O		C	R	O	W	D		N	O	R	A
P	S	Y	C	H		B	E	E	R		O	U	I	
	W	H	I	P	P	E	D	B	U	T	T	E	R	
S	H	A	R	P	E	I		A	G	O				
E	I	R	E		A	L	I	S	T		O	H	M	E
M	P	H		C	H	I	P	P	E	D	B	E	E	F
I	P	O		S	E	N	S	E		C	A	R	A	T
S	O	L		I	N	G	O	D		I	D	O	L	S

43

E	T	A	L		S	C	A	B		S	E	T	T	O
T	U	T	U		T	O	M	E		K	N	E	A	D
U	R	I	S		I	R	I	S		Y	I	E	L	D
I	N	T	H	E	F	A	S	T	P	L	A	N	E	
		I	L	L	S		L	A	C					
A	L	L	A	G	E	S		M	O	B		S	A	G
P	O	O	C	H		H	A	Y		A	U	R	A	
S	A	I	N	T	L	O	U	I	S	P	R	A	M	S
E	T	R	E		E	R	E		L	E	V	E	E	
S	H	E		J	O	B		A	M	U	S	E	R	S
		S	U	N		B	R	I	M					
U	N	C	L	E	B	E	N	S	P	R	I	C	E	
S	N	O	R	E		E	N	O	S		A	S	H	E
A	D	D	A	P		T	I	L	E		C	O	A	L
P	O	E	M	S		A	N	D	S		E	N	D	S

44

M	U	S	H		C	L	I	P		F	L	E	S	H
I	N	C	A		O	O	N	A		A	O	R	T	A
S	P	O	T		N	C	O	S		T	S	A	R	S
S	A	L	E	S	C	O	N	T	A	C	T	S		
M	I	D	D	L	E		E	V	A	C	U	E	E	
E	D	S		U	R	S	A		S	T	A	R	R	Y
		I	N	T	U	N	E		U	E	L	E		
D	R	I	N	K	I	N	G	G	L	A	S	S	E	S
R	I	N	G		S	L	O	A	N	E				
A	C	C	E	S	S		O	S	S	A		C	P	A
M	O	U	N	T	I	E		T	I	A	R	A	S	
	B	U	I	L	D	I	N	G	S	P	E	C	S	
F	L	A	I	L		A	S	I	A		S	A	K	E
L	A	T	T	E		M	A	S	S		E	M	I	T
O	B	E	Y	S		S	K	I	P		S	Y	N	S

45

A	C	M	E		M	R	E	D		J	O	B	S
C	H	E	X		D	E	E	R	E		O	K	R	A
T	A	T	E		E	L	G	I	N		H	I	E	S
A	I	R	C	O	N	D	I	T	I	O	N	E	R	S
S	N	O	U	T	S		S	U	Z	Y	Q			
		T	R	E	A	T		E	L	U	D	E	S
B	A	H	I	A		L	E	A	N		I	R	A	E
O	L	A	V		P	O	R	T	S		N	A	S	A
O	D	I	E		R	U	E	R		O	C	T	E	T
B	A	L	B	O	A		D	I	T	S	Y			
		R	A	T	O	N		E	L	A	I	N	E
T	H	E	A	R	T	F	U	L	D	O	D	G	E	R
S	A	W	N		L	U	R	I	D		A	L	A	N
A	L	E	C		E	S	S	A	Y		M	O	T	S
R	O	S	H		D	E	E	R		S	O	O	T	

46

```
THAW  SLEW  ABOMB
AURA  TUNA  RELEE
USER  ACID  GLINT
THATSRIDICULOUS
    SECT   REY
SAG THERMOS  ACT
TREAT   HOW  SLOW
AREYOUKIDDINGME
ROSE  TIN   FLAME
EWE DINETTE  EAT
    SAC   ARES
DONTMAKEMELAUGH
ALOOP EVAN  TREE
SERVE MELD  IGOR
HOMER PREY  NEMO
```

47

```
SILL  DECI  HANDY
ARIA  ELAN  EIEIO
FEARLESSFOSDICK
ENNEAD  HRH  ALEE
READS  CLAIM
   OHARE  OATERS
SEW  VISA  INDIA
PAINLESSDENTIST
ATSEA PSAT   TEE
TSETSE ORDER
   SPACE  RASTA
ACTS  ELI  INSTEP
SLEEVELESSSHIRT
TORME ETAL  ELSE
ADMIT NYSE  SEER
```

48

```
COKES CABS  SOFA
ADIEU ACUP  OPEC
NICKNAMEFORBUSH
INK HIP FIE  STY
   JADE  ELBA
ILLITERATESMARK
SAABS DER  PLAY
ARR LEADS   EIS
AGAS IMP  HORSE
COMMUNITYCENTER
   ARKS  EURO
STA SAS ABE  MAX
COSTAGAVRASFILM
AUER ERIN  TASTE
BRAY SYNS  ORSON
```

49

```
AUTO  SHU  SCROD
THAR  ROUT WAIVE
MOLE  EBRO ELLEN
SHELFHELP  ALERT
   SLUR  IQTESTS
SCREENSHAVER
ALE AGUA  CRIKEY
GEAR  PYE   DOLE
EMMITT EXPO  LEA
SHUCKERPUNCH
JACKIEO  MOAN
USHER LIPSHTICK
ROADS ACTI  OSLO
ONDIT DEET  LEAK
RESTS ADD   DEMO
```

50

```
WAITASEC BLAMER
ISTHATSO LAMAZE
LITERATE OSIRIS
LAYSOVER WECANT
  BENE CITRATES
GLI  DEMOB
NOTNICE CREATES
ACTEDIN OCANADA
WAYTOGO OHMSLAW
   NAVEL  KMS
BETATRON WEBS
ATRICE TAILLESS
RAILAT RUNSINTO
EGBERT ARKANSAN
DEEDEE PASSKEYS
```

51

```
T I E S █ S I Z E █ L I M E
A R C O █ K N O T █ I N O N
C O U L D A F O O L E D M E
O N A D A T E █ N A D I A █
█ █ █ B E A R █ P T S █ █ █
A B C S █ B R I O █ O G R E
T O O T O O █ S N O █ U A W
W O U L D A B E E N N I C E
A N N █ S R O █ M O U S E R
R E T D █ D O R A █ B E D S
█ █ M E T █ B O N D █ █ █ █
█ S E P I A █ T R I P O L I
S H O U L D A G U E S S E D
R O U T █ M A U L █ S L O E
I T T Y █ S A T E █ T O N S
```

52

```
H E L D █ A L E G █ F U R S
O B O E █ I C I E R █ A T O P
E R I C █ M O R K & M I N D Y
D O S E █ S R A █ P U R E E S
█ █ & I R O N █ L A S █ █ █
V I C T O R █ M I S T A K E N
A L L █ O R S O N █ S L A V E
L O A D █ Y E M E N █ S T O W
E N R O N █ R U R A L █ E K E
T A K E O F F S █ I S L & E R
█ █ █ R L S █ N A D I A █ █
S T I G M A █ B I D █ S L A G
W I L L & G R A C E █ P L U M
A R I A █ O K I E S █ E I R E
N E E D █ N O O R █ █ D E A N
```

53

```
F A R C E █ A L G █ J O A D S
A C U R A █ H U R █ A B N E R
A L I A S █ A L E █ L I N E S
█ U N S T A B L E M A T E S █
█ █ █ H O C █ S N A P █ █ █
T H C █ N T H █ E Y E B A L L
R E E D █ E E G █ N A D I A █
U N D E A D R E C K O N I N G
S C A L P █ L E O █ D O D O █
S E R A P E S █ O A T █ S A S
█ █ E L I S █ L A S █ █ █ █
█ U N S A F E C R A C K E R █
C L E A R █ N R A █ K O R A N
H A S T E █ N A G █ L A I N E
A N T E D █ A P E █ E L C I D
```

54

```
█ H E L G A █ H E R I T A G E
L E V I E S █ I R O N I C A L
E X I S T S █ C R O C P O T S
M A C T R U C K S █ █ U S E █
A N T █ E A R S █ T H I S █ █
Y E S █ A G E █ C O A S T A L
█ █ █ F L E A S A N D T I C S
D I C E █ M A T █ I C E D █ █
Y O U M A K E M E S I C █ █
E N S U R E D █ R E N █ P O W
█ █ T R E Y █ H T T P █ R C A
A V A █ █ T O O T H P I C S █
C A R G O D O C █ L A I D U P
I N D I A I N K █ E S T E R S
D E S T R O Y S █ R E A D S █
```

55

```
S T R E E T C R E D █ B E T A
O R A N G E S O D A █ A A H S
Y O U N G S T O W N █ S S R S
A T L A S T █ K I N G S T O N
█ █ █ O T S █ N O O G I E S
W E N T N U T S █ N O U N █
E R E I █ B U L L █ D I D N T
S O O N █ E P E E S █ T I E R
T O N T O █ E D T V █ A E R O
█ █ C O R M █ S M E A R S O N
B E A R C A T █ E T D █ █
U N R E A S O N █ L E S A G E
M O R T █ C R A B A P P L E S
P L O T █ O R I E N T A T E S
S A T O █ T E L L A S T O R Y
```

```
A R E N A   S L E D   M E M O
T A P I R   C A N I   A D A M
O N I C E   A S T A   L I M A
P I C K O F T H E L I T T E R
      S L O     R U N
L A O   A R T S   P L A S M A
E L M S   G A I T   A G A I N
F L I C K O F T H E W R I S T
T I T A N   T E A L   A L T O
Y E S M A N   S T A G   S Y N
          C O O     T O P
T H I C K O F T H E F I G H T
A I D A   S T O A   I N N E R
O V E R   E E G S   S T A R E
S E A T   S N A P   H A T E S
```

```
S T I R   T O M B   S O N J A
C A R E   O V A L   A D I O S
O P A L   A I D E   N A P E S
F I N E A N D D A N D Y
F R I E N D   R O I   S R A
      A F R O   H E P T A D
S L A B   R O U T   G R A D E
T O L L H O U S E C O O K I E
E I E I O   E T T U   W E I R
E R U P T S   S E L F
P E T   W E B   D O T T I E
      F A R E T H E E W E L L
R A B A T   E R O S   E M I R
A M A Z E   N A P A   E P E E
N A D E R   E P I C   T I D Y
```

```
C O L O N N A   B O B H O P E
U S O T O U R   A P R I C O T
R A Y B U R N   S T U T T E R
A G A S   S I P S   S T A T E
D E L   B E E R   S H H
      G I S   E M U   E U L A
A M N O T   T H A N K S F O R
R O A D T O S I N G A P O R E
T H E M E M O R Y   R O S E S
E S S O   A S I   E M T
      T S R   N O L A   D A H
T A C H O   A G I N   T I N E
S C H E M E D   L I K E N E D
A L A R M E D   E N G L A N D
R U S S E L L   R O B E R T A
```

```
S M E W   C A R B S   A T R A
P A L O   A B O O K   R I I S
A C T O N E S A G E   M E S S
R H O D E S   S E W S   S I E
S U N   P A R T Y   I C O N S
      B A R I   A G I N G
A B D U L   F R E S H N E S S
T R E S   B L O C K   D O U P
C A R T W H E E L   L E N N Y
  T R E A T   A C E R
T W I R L   O N T H E   A D E
H U N   L O B O   O C H R E S
O R G Y   L O S E S H E A R T
U S D A   D E E R E   A C M E
S T O P   E S S E N   D E A R
```

The black squares immediately preceding 24A, 25A, 48A, 50A, 4D, 28D, 29D and 57D should be interpreted as a "block" and read as part of the adjoining answer. For example, 24A = SUNBLOCK, 25A = BLOCK PARTY, etc.

```
F O L K R O C K   A S M A R A
A S O N E M A N   T H E L A W
D E M O T A P E   V O T E I N
S E A B O R N E   S P O R T S
      B O S C     L O O T
S T E E L   R I C H I E
W H O D   J U M B O F R I E S
I O N   G E N E S E T   T I E
M U S C L E C A R S   S E R E
      D A P H N E   A H M E D
  R O C S     P E T R
B A N A N A   H O T T I M E S
E D I S O N   E R N I E E L S
N I C E S T   S T A R K I S T
S I E S T A   A S S E S S E S
```

61

A	B	E	T		P	E	G	S		Z	E	L	I	G
P	E	D	I		E	D	I	T		E	V	I	T	A
S	L	I	D	E	R	U	L	E		P	I	L	O	T
E	L	F	I	N		C	A	T	C	H	L	I	N	E
S	A	Y	E	R	S		S	O	Y					
		D	I	T	C	H		T	R	E	B	L	E	
E	T	A		C	U	R	I	O		F	L	A	W	
N	A	T	I	O	N	A	L	P	A	S	T	I	M	E
O	L	I	O		B	L	A	C	K		P	A	R	
S	E	T	U	P	S		S	L	E	E	P			
		E	U	R		S	T	R	E	A	M			
H	I	T	P	A	R	A	D	E		C	O	R	G	I
E	N	I	A	C		P	I	T	C	H	F	O	R	K
F	R	E	S	H		I	N	T	O		I	D	E	E
T	E	S	T	Y		D	E	A	N		T	E	E	S

62

A	C	H	I	P		P	O	S	H		A	F	A	R
T	E	E	T	H		R	I	P	E		C	A	R	O
E	R	A	T	O		I	L	I	A		E	L	M	O
A	E	R	O	B	I	C	S	C	L	A	S	S		
M	S	T		I	T	E		A	T	M		E	G	G
		P	A	I	L	S		H	O	W	N	O	W	
D	A	D	A		S	I	T	E		N	E	A	L	E
E	X	E	R	C	I	S	E	R	E	G	I	M	E	N
L	O	A	T	H		T	E	R	N		R	E	M	S
O	N	L	Y	I	F		D	O	N	T	S			
S	S	T		L	I	C		R	U	E		B	O	A
	W	E	I	G	H	T	L	I	F	T	I	N	G	
W	H	I	T		U	L	E	E		L	A	C	T	O
S	O	T	O		R	O	N	S		O	D	E	O	N
J	O	H	N		E	E	K	S		N	A	P	P	Y

63

M	A	G	I		A	R	A	B		A	D	A	G	E
O	L	I	N		T	I	N	E		B	E	L	A	Y
C	A	R	T		H	A	N	D		A	M	A	Z	E
K	I	L	O	M	E	T	E	R	S	T	O	N	E	S
		T	I	N	A		I	R	E					
D	E	P	O	S	E		D	D	S		C	H	A	T
O	V	I		D	U	P	E	D		S	P	O	R	E
C	E	N	T	I	M	E	T	E	R	W	O	R	M	S
K	N	E	A	D		R	E	N	E	E		S	E	T
S	T	Y	X		I	S	R		G	R	E	E	D	Y
		Z	A	P		D	I	V	A					
W	H	O	L	E	N	I	N	E	M	E	T	E	R	S
H	O	P	I	S		R	A	C	E		S	L	U	E
E	R	E	C	T		E	T	O	N		U	S	E	R
W	A	C	K	Y		D	O	N	T		P	E	R	T

64

C	C	S		A	L	A	S	K	A		P	O	P	E
O	R	T		N	O	R	M	A	L		F	L	O/P	P
T	I/A	P		D	A	T	I	N	G	S	C	E	N	E
T	S	A	R		N	I	T	S		O	S	A	G	E
A	S	T	I	R		S	T	A	B	S				
		M	A	L	T	E	S	E		A	M	F	M	
S	T	U		B	A	R	N		A	W	H	I	L	E
H	O/I	P	P	I	T	Y		A	T	I/A	S	K	E	T
O	C	T	A	N	E		T	R	I	S		E	W	E
T	K	O	S		S	M	O	O	T	H	S			
		S	T	U	R	M		Y	O	L	K	S		
A	C	H	O	O		S	N	A	P		N	A	N	O
C	H	E	A	P	S	K	A	T	E	S		Z	I/A	G
R	I/A	F	F		R	E	D	I	A	L		E	C	G
O	T	T	S		S	T	O	C	K	Y		S	K	Y

65

O	L	D	P	R	O	S		P	L	E	A	S	E	S
F	O	R	R	E	N	T		R	E	D	L	I	N	E
F	R	I	A	B	L	E		I	C	E	B	A	G	S
R	E	V	I	S	O	R		M	A	N	U	M	I	T
A	L	E	S		W	E	B	E	R		M	E	N	E
M	E	I	E	R		S	U	V		R	E	S	E	T
P	I	N	D	A	R		Z	A	N	I	N	E	S	S
			D	A	Z	Z	L	E	S					
S	P	O	R	A	D	I	C		W	E	T	M	O	P
H	A	V	E	R		P	U	B		S	H	A	N	A
O	P	E	S		O	C	T	A	L		E	G	E	R
T	O	R	P	E	D	O		R	E	G	R	E	S	S
P	O	L	I	C	E	D		T	O	R	O	N	T	O
A	S	A	R	U	L	E		A	V	E	S	T	A	N
R	E	P	E	A	L	S		B	I	G	E	A	R	S

66

S	T	U	C	C	O	■	C	O	L	D	■	S	P	A
C	A	L	L	O	N	■	L	U	A	U	■	T	A	X
U	P	T	O	S	C	R	A	T	C	H	■	E	L	I
F	I	R	S	■	E	A	R	L	Y	■	H	A	M	S
F	R	A	U	D	■	S	E	E	■	C	A	D	■	■
■	■	R	I	G	H	T	T	O	L	I	F	E	R	■
F	O	R	E	G	O	E	S	■	D	E	R	A	T	E
A	R	I	■	I	T	S	■	P	E	R	■	S	R	A
I	N	F	A	N	T	■	C	L	O	I	S	T	E	R
L	E	F	T	T	O	C	H	A	N	C	E	■	■	■
■	■	R	O	O	■	R	A	Y	■	S	A	B	L	E
S	P	A	M	■	P	E	N	A	L	■	L	A	I	T
E	L	F	■	D	O	W	N	T	O	E	A	R	T	H
R	E	F	■	A	L	E	E	■	O	R	N	E	R	Y
B	A	S	■	Y	E	L	L	■	P	E	T	R	E	L

67

S	H	E	S	■	R	A	S	P	■	B	L	A	Z	E
C	A	P	T	■	I	R	A	E	■	E	A	G	E	R
A	L	S	O	■	N	I	N	E	■	E	X	E	R	T
B	L	O	W	A	G	A	S	K	E	T	■	D	O	E
S	E	M	E	L	E	■	■	S	A	L	S	■	■	■
■	■	■	O	R	E	M	■	R	E	C	E	S	S	■
A	S	T	R	O	■	T	A	R	T	■	O	D	I	E
F	L	Y	O	F	F	T	H	E	H	A	N	D	L	E
R	A	P	T	■	R	A	R	E	■	B	E	A	L	S
O	T	O	O	L	E	■	E	L	S	A	■	■	■	■
■	■	R	E	D	O	■	■	I	C	E	A	G	E	■
P	T	A	■	G	O	B	A	L	L	I	S	T	I	C
O	I	L	E	R	■	E	R	I	K	■	T	A	L	L
S	T	A	R	E	■	S	O	M	E	■	E	L	L	A
T	O	R	R	E	■	E	D	E	N	■	R	E	S	T

68

B	Y	A	■	S	P	I	C	E	■	O	M	A	H	A
R	O	T	■	O	R	S	O	N	■	M	A	G	I	C
O	O	O	■	B	E	A	R	T	H	E	C	O	S	T
O	H	M	S	■	M	A	R	S	A	L	A	■	■	■
D	O	I	N	G	O	K	■	J	E	W	E	L	S	■
S	O	C	I	A	L	■	A	T	I	T	■	L	E	E
■	■	P	L	A	I	T	S	■	■	I	B	E	T	■
T	H	E	E	A	R	T	H	A	N	D	M	A	R	S
E	E	L	S	■	T	O	R	E	U	P	■	■	■	■
A	M	A	■	W	H	Y	S	■	E	R	A	S	E	S
M	I	L	I	E	U	■	■	B	D	A	L	T	O	N
■	■	M	A	R	S	H	A	L	■	A	R	C	O	■
C	L	E	A	R	T	H	E	A	I	R	■	E	E	O
R	I	N	G	O	■	A	R	E	N	A	■	A	N	T
O	L	D	E	N	■	H	E	D	G	E	■	K	E	Y

69

N	A	B	■	I	A	M	I	■	A	T	W	O	R	K
E	R	R	■	S	L	A	M	■	R	O	O	M	I	E
W	H	Y	D	O	E	S	A	■	M	E	N	A	G	E
T	A	C	I	T	■	■	C	L	A	P	T	R	A	P
S	T	E	P	O	U	T	■	A	N	I	■	■	■	■
■	■	■	P	S	Y	C	H	I	C	H	A	V	E	■
S	A	N	P	E	D	R	O	■	■	K	A	L	E	L
P	U	C	E	■	A	A	R	O	N	■	N	O	R	I
I	T	A	G	O	■	F	R	O	M	A	T	O	Z	■
T	O	A	S	K	Y	O	U	F	O	R	■	■	■	■
■	■	A	E	R	■	F	R	A	P	P	E	S	■	■
A	N	A	L	Y	S	T	S	■	■	P	A	R	M	A
D	E	B	U	G	S	■	Y	O	U	R	N	A	M	E
A	V	E	N	U	E	■	N	I	S	I	■	T	E	N
M	A	L	A	Y	S	■	E	L	A	L	■	E	T	S

70

■	P	A	U	L	E	T	T	E	■	G	O	F	A	R
T	A	R	N	I	S	H	E	S	■	E	V	I	T	A
W	O	O	D	S	T	O	C	K	■	T	A	R	O	T
I	L	L	■	T	A	U	■	I	N	S	T	E	P	S
T	I	L	L	E	D	■	S	M	I	T	E	S	■	■
■	■	■	A	D	O	■	H	O	N	I	■	T	H	E
A	M	B	I	■	■	M	A	D	E	P	R	O	U	D
N	O	U	N	S	■	A	N	O	■	S	I	N	G	E
T	H	R	E	A	D	I	N	G	■	■	T	E	E	N
E	R	N	■	D	O	N	E	■	B	I	Z	■	■	■
■	■	S	A	T	U	R	N	■	A	N	Y	M	A	N
T	R	I	B	O	R	O	■	C	T	N	■	A	D	E
R	I	D	E	S	■	A	S	H	T	A	B	U	L	A
A	L	E	T	A	■	D	E	A	L	T	O	V	E	R
M	E	S	S	Y	■	S	C	R	E	E	N	E	R	■

71

```
A H A B   P H A T   R A P I D
G Y R O   L E C H   E L E N A
A D I A   A M M O   L E A F Y
P R E T T Y P E N N Y   C O S
E A S E U P     G O O S E
      D R E A D   S N A P P Y
A R P   I N V A D E   M I L O
L E A R N   O N E   R E P A Y
I D L E   O N T A P E   E N O
T O M A T O   E D U C E
    P L A Z A   L A N C E S
L E I   P E N C I L P O I N T
O X L I P   G A S P   U L E E
S P O K E   U G L I   G I M P
T O T E D   S E E N   H A Y S
```

72

```
A P A C E   F I R S T   B U G
R A D A R   A L O H A   U R I
P R O D I G A L S O N   M B A
    R C A   U S E   S P A N
R E P E A L   M I S S P E N T
O P U S   I V E   A R R A S
S I S   A L E   E T H I C
S C H E M E R   T R I G R A M
    K A B O B   T A B   O L E
A R I S E   H U M   A P E S
G E N E R A T E   C U R S E S
A S P S   G A R   A N I
V O L   J A B B E R W O C K Y
E R A   A T L A S   O S H E A
S T Y   R E E L S   N E I G H
```

73

```
D A S H   R I C O   E X A C T
E S A I   O V I D   E E R I E
G I L L   D E A D L Y S I N S
A D E L L E   O L E O   D E T
S E S S I O N   Y A R D
    O L S O N   N E A R B Y
T A F F Y   T O T O   Y A L E
H E A R   S E V E N   S P U N
A R L O   E D E N   S I T E S
R O A M E R   L O R E N
    E V E N   R E L A P S E
S N O   E N I D   E L W O O D
L I T T L E F O Y S   E R O S
A N T S Y   T R U E   E T T E
M A S O N   Y A M S   K O H L
```

74

```
S C A R F   C O M S   A V I V
C R U E L   H O O T   T A T E
H(UM)PTYD(UM)PTY   E C O L
U P A   T A S S E L   D U R(UM)
S L I P O N   T E D I(UM)
S E R E   G A L   T O R P I D
    W A M P(UM)   S T(UM)P Y
S O D   S E E P A G E   P O E
T H(UM)B S   S P A D E
D O D O E S   (UM)P S   L I L T
    A N T O N   C A D M I(UM)
C E D E   M I C M A C   G A B
A L(UM)S   A L(UM)I N(UM)F O I L
B A D U   L E I S   E R O S E
S L(UM)P   I S N T   N O D E S
```

75

```
O H M E   S C R E A M E D A T
N A I L   T R A M P O L I N E
D R A B   R O T T E N I D E A
E M M A   A C E S   T H I N K
P O I   I N K   S H U N T S
O N H A N D   J A I L
S I E N A   F O L L Y   Q E D
I C A N T S A Y F O R S U R E
T A T   T O S C A   E D I N A
    H A T E   I N S T I R
Y A P P E R   T N T   E E S
A W E E K   G R I N   A G F A
W H E N I N R O M E   N O O N
L I T T L E O N E S   T O R T
S T E A L A K I S S   E D D A
```

The New York Times

Crossword Puzzles

The #1 name in crosswords

Available at your local bookstore or online at nytimes.com/nytstore

Coming Soon!

Simply Sunday Crosswords	0-312-34243-8	$6.95/$9.95 Can.
Beach Blanket Crosswords	0-312-34250-0	$6.95/$9.95 Can.
Large-Print Crosswords for Your Bedside	0-312-34245-4	$10.95/$15.95 Can.
More Quick Crosswords	0-312-34246-2	$6.95/$9.95 Can.
Lazy Weekend Crosswords	0-312-34247-0	$11.95/$16.95 Can.
Will Shortz's Greatest Hits	0-312-34242-X	$8.95/$12.95 Can.
Tough Crosswords Vol. 13	0-312-34240-3	$10.95/$15.95 Can.
Daily Crosswords Vol. 70	0-312-34239-X	$9.95/$14.95 Can.
Crosswords for the Weekend	0-312-34332-9	$9.95/$14.95 Can.
Easy as Pie Crosswords	0-312-34331-0	$6.95/$9.95 Can.

Special Editions

Super Sunday Crosswords	0-312-33115-0	$10.95/$15.95 Can.
Will Shortz's Funniest Crosswords Vol. 2	0-312-33960-7	$9.95/$14.95 Can.
Will Shortz's Funniest Crosswords	0-312-32489-8	$9.95/$14.95 Can.
Will Shortz's Favorite Sundays	0-312-32488-X	$9.95/$14.95 Can.
Crosswords for a Brain Workout	0-312-32610-6	$6.95/$9.95 Can.
Crosswords to Boost Your Brainpower	0-312-32033-7	$6.95/$9.95 Can.
Crossword All-Stars	0-312-31004-8	$9.95/$14.95 Can.
Will Shortz's Favorites	0-312-30613-X	$9.95/$14.95 Can.
Ultimate Omnibus	0-312-31622-4	$6.95/$9.95 Can.

Daily Crosswords

Monday to Friday Vol. 2	0-312-31459-0	$9.95/$14.95 Can.
Monday through Friday	0-312-30058-1	$9.95/$14.95 Can.
Daily Crosswords Vol. 69	0-312-33956-9	$9.95/$14.95 Can.
Daily Crosswords Vol. 68	0-312-33434-6	$9.95/$14.95 Can.
Daily Crosswords Vol. 67	0-312-32437-5	$9.95/$14.95 Can.
Daily Crosswords Vol. 66	0-312-32436-7	$9.95/$14.95 Can.
Daily Crosswords Vol. 65	0-312-32034-5	$9.95/$14.95 Can.
Daily Crosswords Vol. 64	0-312-31458-2	$9.95/$14.95 Can.
Daily Crosswords Vol. 63	0-312-30947-3	$9.95/$14.95 Can.

Easy Crosswords

Easy Crosswords Vol. 6	0-312-33957-7	$10.95/$15.95 Can.
Easy Crosswords Vol. 5	0-312-32438-3	$9.95/$14.95 Can.
Easy Crosswords Vol. 4	0-312-30448-X	$9.95/$14.95 Can.
Easy Crosswords Vol. 3	0-312-28912-X	$9.95/$14.95 Can.

Tough Crosswords

Tough Crosswords Vol. 12	0-312-32442-1	$10.95/$15.95 Can.
Tough Crosswords Vol. 11	0-312-31456-6	$10.95/$15.95 Can.
Tough Crosswords Vol. 10	0-312-30060-3	$10.95/$15.95 Can.

Sunday Crosswords

Sunday Crosswords Vol. 30	0-312-33538-5	$9.95/$14.95 Can.
Sunday Crosswords Vol. 29	0-312-32038-8	$9.95/$14.95 Can.
Sunday Crosswords Vol. 28	0-312-30515-X	$9.95/$14.95 Can.
Sunday Crosswords Vol. 27	0-312-28414-4	$9.95/$14.95 Can.

Large-Print Crosswords

Large-Print Will Shortz's Favorite Crosswords	0-312-33959-3	$10.95/$15.95 Can.
Large-Print Big Book of Easy Crosswords	0-312-33958-5	$12.95/$18.95 Can.
Large-Print Big Book of Holiday Crosswords	0-312-33092-8	$12.95/$18.95 Can.
Large-Print Crosswords for Your Coffeebreak	0-312-33109-6	$10.95/$15.95 Can.
Large-Print Crosswords for a Brain Workout	0-312-32612-2	$10.95/$15.95 Can.
Large-Print Crosswords to Boost Your Brainpower	0-312-32037-X	$11.95/$17.95 Can.
Large-Print Easy Omnibus	0-312-32439-1	$12.95/$18.95 Can.
Large-Print Daily Vol. 2	0-312-33111-8	$10.95/$15.95 Can.
Large-Print Daily Crosswords	0-312-31457-4	$10.95/$15.95 Can.
Large-Print Omnibus Vol. 5	0-312-32036-1	$12.95/$18.95 Can.
Large-Print Omnibus Vol. 4	0-312-30514-1	$12.95/$18.95 Can.

Omnibus

Crossword Challenge	0-312-33951-8	$12.95/$18.95 Can.
Big Book of Holiday Crosswords	0-312-33533-4	$11.95/$17.95 Can.
Crosswords for a Lazy Afternoon	0-312-33108-8	$11.95/$17.95 Can.
Tough Omnibus Vol. 1	0-312-32441-3	$11.95/$14.95 Can.
Easy Omnibus Vol. 3	0-312-33537-7	$11.95/$17.95 Can.
Easy Omnibus Vol. 2	0-312-32035-3	$11.95/$17.95 Can.
Easy Omnibus Vol. 1	0-312-30513-3	$11.95/$17.95 Can.
Daily Omnibus Vol. 14	0-312-33534-2	$11.95/$17.95 Can.
Daily Omnibus Vol. 13	0-312-32031-0	$11.95/$17.95 Can.
Daily Omnibus Vol. 12	0-312-30511-7	$11.95/$17.95 Can.
Sunday Omnibus Vol. 8	0-312-32440-5	$11.95/$17.95 Can.
Sunday Omnibus Vol. 7	0-312-30950-3	$11.95/$17.95 Can.
Sunday Omnibus Vol. 6	0-312-28913-8	$11.95/$17.95 Can.

Variety Puzzles

Acrostic Puzzles Vol. 9	0-312-30949-X	$9.95/$14.95 Can.
Sunday Variety Puzzles	0-312-30059-X	$9.95/$14.95 Can.

Portable Size Format

Crosswords for a Rainy Day	0-312-33952-6	$6.95/$9.95 Can.
Crosswords for Stress Relief	0-312-33953-4	$6.95/$9.95 Can.
Crosswords to Beat the Clock	0-312-33954-2	$6.95/$9.95 Can.
Quick Crosswords	0-312-33114-2	$6.95/$9.95 Can.
More Sun, Sand and Crosswords	0-312-33112-6	$6.95/$9.95 Can.
Planes, Trains and Crosswords	0-312-33113-4	$6.95/$9.95 Can.
Cup of Tea and Crosswords	0-312-32435-9	$6.95/$9.95 Can.
Crosswords for Your Bedside	0-312-32032-9	$6.95/$9.95 Can.
Beach Bag Crosswords	0-312-31455-8	$6.95/$9.95 Can.
Crosswords for the Work Week	0-312-30952-X	$6.95/$9.95 Can.
T.G.I.F. Crosswords	0-312-33116-9	$6.95/$9.95 Can.
Super Saturday	0-312-30604-0	$6.95/$9.95 Can.
Sun, Sand and Crosswords	0-312-30076-X	$6.95/$9.95 Can.
Crosswords to Exercise Your Brain	0-312-33536-9	$6.95/$9.95 Can.
Crosswords for Your Breakfast Table	0-312-33535-0	$6.95/$9.95 Can.

For Young Solvers

New York Times on the Web Crosswords for Teens	0-312-28911-1	$6.95/$9.95 Can.
Outrageous Crossword Puzzles and Word Games for Kids	0-312-28915-1	$6.95/$9.95 Can.
More Outrageous Crossword Puzzles for Kids	0-312-30062-X	$6.95/$9.95 Can.

St. Martin's Griffin